CARDINAL POINTS LITERARY JOURNAL
VOLUME 5

a project of
www.StoSvet.net
cp@StoSvet.net

Editor-in chief
Oleg Woolf (1954-2011)

Editors:
Irina Mashinski
Robert Chandler
Boris Dralyuk

Issue Editor: Boris Dralyuk

Publicity and Marketing: Alex Cigale
Book and Cover Design: Jonathan Penton
Original Front and Back Cover Design: Sergey Samsonov
Interior Art and Graphics: Gregory Kowalsky
Proofreader: Bernd Sauermann

ISBN-13: 978-1-941196-15-1

published in collaboration with
MadHat Press
PO Box 8364
Asheville, NC 28814
www.MadHat-Press.com

CARDINAL POINTS

JOURNAL

VOLUME 5

DEDICATED TO DESTALINIZATION OF THE AIR

StoSvet Press
New York, New York

/

MadHat Press
Asheville, North Carolina

This issue of Cardinal Points is dedicated to the memory of the brilliant translators Stanley Mitchell (1932-2011), Michael Henry Heim (1943-2012), F. D. Reeve (1928-2013), Daniel Weissbort (1935-2013), and George Kline (1921-2014), as well as the legendary poets Natalya Gorbanevskaya (1936-2013), Stanisław Barańczak (1946-2014), Nina Cassian (1924-2014), Maxine Kumin (1925-2014), Inna Lisnyanskaya (1928-2014), and Mark Strand (1934-2014). These men and women set moral standards for several generations of readers, students, and colleagues; they are paragons of professionalism and open-mindedness.

STOSVET

PRESS

CONTENTS

POETRY

THE COMPASS TRANSLATION AWARD: RUSSIAN POETRY IN ENGLISH

Poetry

Konstantin Batyushkov
Translated from the Russian by Peter France

FROM THE GREEK ANTHOLOGY

I

In nothingness's gloomy mansion
Oh woman unforgettable! Accept from me
Tears and despairing cries on your cold tombstone,
  Roses ephemeral as you!
  All is in vain. Eternal darkness
Will not give up your ever-grieving shadow;
We cannot call you back from envious Hades.
Here all is dumb and cold; here nothing speaks.
My funeral torch only reveals the blackness...
What have you done, you governors of heaven?
Say, why does beauty have so short a life?
But mother earth, take these my bitter tears,
Take her who sleeps, the faded flower of spring,
And may she rest in hospitable shade.

Konstantin Batyushkov, trans. Peter France

II

Witnesses of my love and sorrow,
Youthful roses, damp with tears!
Deck with your wreaths the modest cottage
Where my beloved shuns our eyes.
Remain, sweet wreaths, and do not wither!
But if she comes, pour out on her
All your sweet odour, and once more
Water with tears her lovely tresses.
May she stand wondering, and sigh;
And you, flowers, with your fragrant breath,
Water with tears my dear one's tresses.

V

Where is the fame, the beauty that undid you?
The busy streets, the happy citizens?
Where are the sumptuous halls, the noble temples,
The gold, the tessera that shone in them?
Alas, great many-pillared Corinth, gone forever ,
Your very ash is scattered through the fields,
All is a void, we only cry to heaven,
The halcyon alone grieves in the mist!

VII

Let's hide forever from men's envious eyes
The ardent raptures and the swoon of passion.
How sweet a kiss in the unspeaking night,
How sweet love's business and its hidden pleasures!

VIII

I love the smile playing on Laisa's lips,
Her talk that captivates the heart, but dearer
Than everything to me are her shy looks
And in her eyes the tears of sudden sorrow.
Last night at twilight, overcome by passion,
I knelt again before her, spoke of love:
    My kisses led her on to pleasure
    On the soft couch laid out for us...
    I burned with love, she stood unmoving...
    But suddenly grew pale, despondent
    And tears came flooding from her eyes!
Taken aback, I pressed her to my bosom:
"What's troubling you, my dear, what's troubling you?"
"Don't worry, it is nothing, God's my witness;
    Just one thought troubles me", she said:
"You men are faithless, and... I feel afraid."

IX

Is it for you to mourn your young days gone?
    You are as beautiful as ever
        And with the passing years
Ever more captivating to your lover.
I do not prize an inexperienced beauty,
Unskilled in all the mysteries of love;
Her modest gaze is lifeless and unspeaking,
Her timid kisses by no feeling moved.
    But you, love's empress, could awaken
    An answering passion in a stone
    And in your autumn days you quicken
    The flame that through the bloodstream flows.

X

Alas! These eyes bedimmed by weeping,
The hours of suffering in these hollow cheeks,
   They don't awaken your compassion—
   A cruel smile plays on your lips...
These are the bitter fruits of passion,
Sad fruits of passion that no joy relieves,
   The fruits of love, worthy of favour
And not the fate that so benumbs the heart...
Alas! Like sudden lightning up in heaven,
   Passions eat up our early years,
   Perfidiously, they leave us cheerless,
   Afflicted by never-ending tears.
But you, my beauty, you whose love is dearer
To me than all my youth and happiness,
   Take pity on me... and I will recover,
   Younger and brighter than I was.

XII

Life is exhausted in my frozen heart:
An end to struggle and to everything!
Eros and Aphrodite, you tormentors,
Hear my last words, my melancholy!
I fade away, yet undergo new tortures,
   Half dead, but not consumed,
I fade away, my love is still as ardent,
   And without hope I die!
So on the altar, 'round the sacrifice,
   The fire grows pale and dwindles,
Then, flaring up before it dies,
   Is quenched amid the ashes.

And I don't leave the room. I stay,
hoping I might postpone his death.

Wojciech Bonowicz
Translated from the Polish by Piotr Florczyk

THE BEGINNING

At night the whistling for the dogs
sounds clearer. I was afraid
of the howling. Very. When I was
little every gale would take away

my room. Between the blocks
the air went mad sometimes.
By then I had an enemy and he
didn't scare me but the wailing did.

Wojciech Bonowicz, trans. Piotr Florczyk

THE BAD KNOWS

The bad will warm them. The bad will embrace
this rally of the forsaken and give it a sense.
The bad likes to watch how nothingness thickens
when fire's lit. The bad knows:

those who mumble and those who shout
are brothers. Fear skips between them—
fear is their song. The bad knows:
it's been writing the lyrics all night long.

CONTENT

Do I speak as if I knew?
I don't know.

The day is bright
and dark.

I lean forward to see better

and see
that a face
hasn't burned out.

Earth sky

and a face
between them.

Wojciech Bonowicz, trans. Piotr Florczyk

Private History

"It doesn't hurt," she says in her sleep. And I know she's talking
to me. Then she goes back to the place designated

by fear. A cat and a pigeon a moment before
the chase and the escape. A flower swallowed in silence

and fingers writing in the air the three first
letters of the day. It doesn't hurt. "It will," I say.

Edwin Frank

SNAKE TRAIN

—after Khlebnikov

We settled in our ochre houndstooth seats
And stirred our drinks.   We talked about the Good,
Damned Cowardice, praised Courage, and said we would

Have done much better to have lived when war
Was decent, when there was something to die for—
The future perfect, if not a lasting peace—

Or not to have been born. The high-speed train
Ran smooth as our reckonings.   We sat upon
The observation deck beneath a green

Plexiglas bubble that dulled the glare and sheen
Of dusk into a botch of blacks and whites
As the train slid west and the last trace of light

Twisted, crumpled, and powdered like a scrap
Of burning paper.   The conversation lapsed.
The train was pleasant, not too old or new,

And carpeted in red, car followed car
Like scenes in a play or shops in a bazaar,
While hardly swaying we moved as quickly as

A match flame sizzles through dry summer grass.
Evenings, we lingered in the dining car,
Dropped ashes on the tablecloth and stole

23

Spotty carnations, yellow silverware,
And tipped a lot.   The canned gentility
Charmed us, claimed us.... Feeling kind and free,

I looked around.   The other passengers
Had fallen asleep.   They smiled maliciously
Like dolls, or lay there stony-faced,

While someone muttered something in a dream.
I looked outside—night's eddying blue-blacks,
Streaking lights, still patches of light fog—

And thought I glimpsed the shiny pulse of gills
Or giant outline of a black-gloved fist
Studded with stars, the knuckles bunched like hills—

Imagine! A winged dragon! It tore along
Beside us with the vague, furtive smirk
Of someone who enjoys a private joke

Stretched across its heart-shaped snout.   A book
Lay open on its head in place of hair,
And its scales were clear as the gray windowpanes

Of city halls, so I could see the veins'
Inky designs, like baroque emblems where
The virtues and the vices strut their stuff,

And its scorpion tail hovering above.
"It must be going a good seventy,"
I thought, as it lumbered heavily

Past us on its little baby's legs.
Then baring the whites of its sharp teeth,
It spread its wings until they filled the sky

Like a wedding canopy trimmed with razor wire
And rose. The train jerked back under its bulk
Then jolted forward, sped on by the wings,

As I slammed against the seat in front of me
And hit the floor, meeting my friend's shocked
Eyes of blame and threat. The beast's jaws sheared

The plastic top, but everyone took his seat
And settled back in with a snore or sneeze
Full of experience and expertise,

While I thought, Saint George, of you, and how you stood
Undaunted by the dragon's brawn and airs
Until you saw the earth drink the black blood

Of its death wound. The thought did me no good.
The beast bore down—my heart banged in my side—
And craning my neck, I saw it chomp a bright

Young lawyer screaming in its teeth , "No right!"
And lunge towards me. I nearly died.
But taking advantage of a twist in the tail,

My friend and I jumped into the night.
Under the branches of a cottonwood,
Beside a muddy creek, we pitched camp.

Antelope, jackrabbit, gopher, grass
For food. We kept alive as a spoken word
Or campfire's ash and smoldering peat

Keep, for a little while, a little heat.
But every one of that commonsensical lot
Was eaten by the dragon on the spot.

Alexander Kushner
Translated from the Russian by Olga Zaslavsky

THE ROCK

Where is that rock,
that rock, that rock,
from which the trembling bodies
were thrown
down,
down,
clinging to a low shrub, as if it were a cornice molding?
The rock must still be there, waiting.
Oh, to see it, to climb to the top,
and birds of prey circle above.

And underneath I hope to see
a glittering sea, a sea, a sea,
and not the usual mess of tourist waste
and private shame.
Or did I take it for the rock that Sappho found
to drink oblivion, not gradually, like most of us, but in one gulp?

And, then, I read
and read
and read
how today's philosopher from France
arrived in Greece and chose a rock,
but was distracted by barking dogs,
so he sat at its edge, then crawled away and sprawled on his back.

Alexander Kushner, trans. Olga Zaslavsky

And aren't we falling into an abyss,
stumbling at every moment,
together, each owned by a fear that is his?
No matter how many books we read,
the reading hardly helps us find
protection from a deathly cry inside.
We long to keep and keep and keep that cry
for, poor thing,
It's so alive!

Osip Mandelstam
Translated from the Russian by Peter France

BATYUSHKOV

Like a flâneur with a magic cane,
tender Batyushkov lives at my place—
wanders down Zamostie lanes,
sniffs a rose, sings Zafna's praise.

Not for a moment believing that we
could be separated, I bowed to him:
I shake his brightly gloved cold hand
in an envious delirium.

He smiled at me. "Thank you," I said,
so shy I could not find the words:
No one commands such curves of sound,
never was there such speech of waves.

With oblique words he made us feel
the wealth and torments that we share—
the buzz of verse-making, brotherhood's bell
and the harmonies of pouring tears.

And the mourner of Tasso answered me:
"I am not yet used to eulogy;
I only cooled my tongue by chance
on the grape-flesh of poetry."

All right, raise your eyebrows in surprise,
city dweller and city dweller's friend—
like blood samples, from glass to glass
keep pouring your eternal dreams.

June 18, 1932

ARIOSTO

The cleverest man in Italy, untroubled,
suave Ariosto feels a little hoarse.
He revels in his catalogue of fish,
peppers the oceans with malicious babble.

Like a musician playing on ten cymbals,
he tirelessly snaps off the thread of tales,
not knowing his own way, he pulls all ways
his mixed-up story of chivalric scandals.

On the cicadas' tongue, a captivating air—
Pushkinian sadness with southern conceit—
he catches Orlando in a web of lies
and shudders, feeling utterly transfixed.

And to the sea he says: Roar without thought.
And to the maiden on the rock: Lie bare...
Tell us more tales, then, we can't get enough,
as long as blood flows in us and ears hear...

O town of lizards, where there's not a soul!
If only you could give us more like him,
Callous Ferrara... Hurry, yet again,
as long as blood flows in us, tell us tales...

It's cold in Europe, dark in Italy.
Power is repulsive, like a barber's hands.
But he still lords it better, cunningly,
and out through the wide open window sends

a smile to the hill lambs, and to the monk
on donkey-back, and to the ducal troops,
silly from wine and garlic and the plague,
and to the child that sleeps among blue flies.

But I love his unbridled freedom, love
his foolish language, sweetly salted tongue,
and the enchanting clash of double sounds—
I fear to cut the pearl from the bivalve.

Suave Ariosto, who knows, an age will pass—
and into a single wide fraternal blue
we'll pour your azure and our own black sea.
We too were there. And there we drank the mead.

May 4-6, 1933, Stary Krym

Osip Mandelstam, trans. Peter France

BLACK EARTH

Too black, too much indulged, living in clover,
all little withers, all air, all loving care,
all crumbling and all massing in a choir—
damp clods of soil, my freedom and my earth...

With early plowing it is black to blueness,
and unarmed labor here is glorified—
a thousand hills plowed open wide to say it—
circumference is not all circumscribed.

And yet the earth is blunder and obtuseness—
no swaying it, even on bended knee:
its rotting flute gives sharpness to the hearing,
its morning clarinet harrows the ear.

How sweet the fat earth's pressure on the plow,
how the spring turns the steppe to its advantage...
my greetings then, black earth: be strong, look out—
black eloquence of wordlessness in labor.

April 1935

"Deep in the hill the idol sits unmoving..."

Deep in the hill the idol sits unmoving
in his unbounded, caring, happy chambers,
while from his neck the grease of jewels drips,
protecting dreams that ebb and flow.

When he was a boy, a peacock was his playmate;
they fed him on a rainbow of the Indies
and gave him milk out of rose-colored clay
and never spared the cochineal.

Lulled into sleep the bone is knitted up,
the knees, the hands, the shoulders all made human.
He smiles with his own quietest of smiles,
thinking with bone and feeling with his forehead,
attempting to recall his human features.

December 1936

Osip Mandelstam, trans. Peter France

"ARMED WITH THE EYESIGHT OF THIN-WAISTED WASPS..."

Armed with the eyesight of thin-waisted wasps
that suck at the earth's axis, the earth's axis,
I sense it all, all that I ever saw,
and vainly, word for word, try to recall it...

I make no pictures, neither do I sing
nor draw the black-voiced bow across the string:
I only suck on life, and love to envy
the wasps, so potent and so sly.

Oh if I too could one day be impelled
by summer's heat and by the air's sharp practice
to feel, as I avoided sleep and death,
earth's axis, yes, to penetrate earth's axis...

February 8, 1937

THREE PORTRAITS WITHOUT FRAMES

Lev Ozerov
Translated from the Russian by Boris Dralyuk

ALISA KOONEN (1889-1974)

The name Alisa Koonen
is like a house with many windows,
a temple with many columns.
Back then the name was here, there—
now on Bolshaya Bronnaya,
then on Tverskoy Boulevard,
before that, in the Chamber Theater.

I once saw Koonen walking down Tverskoy.
Her movement was slow and melodic,
befitting a tragic actress.
This was after the theater's last show,
after all the applause,
after all the afters.
This was after the letters
her husband Tairov had sent
up to the highest powers—
into that deep
irresponsible abyss
from which
there was never
response.

It was a gloomy, wind-swept day,
with clouds gathering over the theater.
The night before, Koonen had played
Adrienne Lecouvreur once more.
And now—never again.
The night before, she'd watched in pain,
although she had tried not to look,
as the curtain fell
one last time—
it was as if a pall
were falling on her life,
as if the little sash
inside the crematorium were drawing closed,
and the deceased were entering the flames.

There would be no more Adrienne,
no Anita, and no more Phaedra,
no Abbie, no Emma Bovary.
Ah, the life of an actor!
The roles one plays,
but most of all—
the roles one hasn't played.
One longs for them.
They hurt, these unplayed roles,
like phantom limbs.

Koonen is walking down the boulevard.
Some passerby abuses a guitar.
Some lady comes along, carrying a parrot.
Koonen? Is it really Koonen?
Yes, it's Koonen! No mistake. It's Adrienne!
The Theater's banned now. The stage is boarded up—
crossed planks across the door. But life goes on,
as does that voice—an echo from an empty well.

Koonen is walking down the boulevard.
Yes, right before my eyes...
Coming to meet her
(yes, seeking her, drawn towards her
all the way through life),
a man is hurrying along, not quite at a run.
This never changes. He is slightly stooped,
dressed smartly, but he looks shaken.
Approaching Koonen carefully, he bends,
kisses her hand. This never changes—
throughout his life. Gray locks of hair aspire to cover
the ivory bald spot on the maestro's head,
but cannot cover it completely. Life
has been ruptured. But it's Tairov, isn't it?
All gone. And he had wanted
to stage *Macbeth*. And his *Macbeth*
went straight to hell.

Tairov walks up to Koonen
as if for the first time
after a long, long separation. He's in love—
a love that's mad, tender, hopeless.
He speaks so quietly. She doesn't say a word.
She doesn't blink. She simply looks at him
intently, sadly, with surprise.
He turns beside her on his heel, as if inviting
her to dance. But it's no time for dancing.
He takes her by the arm. And there they go—
slow, sad, melodic.

Lev Ozerov, trans. Boris Dralyuk

I cannot tear my eyes away.
Yes, really, this all happened—
before my eyes.
There they go—quite real—a couple,
There they go—half-real—a vision,
Off they go—unreal—a dream.
Off they go into the fog, forever,
into the distance,
into what can't be known or measured.

VSEVOLOD MEYERHOLD (1874-1940)

A man runs in,
and on his heels—a breeze,
heralding genius.
It fans everyone in the foyer.
No one says, "He's here now."
Everyone feels his presence.
Nobody says: "He has arrived."
Everyone feels: "He's here."
He takes his scarf off on the go—
a general bow—
throws off his coat,
and someone grabs it, carries it away somewhere.
The day begins.
"Let's get to work,
A List of Benefits—
Yury Karlovich Olesha,
please give him a warm welcome."
Meyerhold concentrates, gliding through space,
seeking the right tonality,
and sparkles with the warm gray blueness of his eyes,
their bluish greenness.
The eyes can grow dark in anger.
The eyelids drop majestically.
The backstage smells of planks,
wood-chips, perfume,
Griboyedov's verses.
Disheveled, smoky-gray,
he quickly removes his jacket.

Two actors are on stage beside him.
One has to hit the other.
"Wrong!" says Meyerhold.
He doesn't work on the one doing the hitting—
he grabs the one taking the hit.
Squatting, bending sideways,
he raises his hands in defense
against the hitter.
"Again, again!
You're hitting a person,
not chopping firewood.
There's a difference!
We'll come back to this."
The scenes have yet to fall in place;
They're still
just getting used to one another.
Meyerhold is getting used to them
and sculpting a performance.
It comes together in the strangest fashion—
out of guesswork, non sequiturs,
everything we find hard to predict.
I took a liking to the mystery of rehearsals,
knew everyone by name:
Raikh, Babanova, Shtraukh,
Martinson, Shostakovich, Garin,
Shabalin, Ilyinsky, and others—
sharp, vivid, unforgettable.
I hear the famous:
"Ulalume! The great Ulalume's arrived!"
What words!
I remember them from early youth.

I saw Meyerhold at other times:
stepping out on stage, summoned by the audience;
looking over the theater building
on Triumfalnaya Square;
talking to Olesha
about *Hamlet.*
Meyerhold is deprived of a theater,
deprived of a home,
deprived of life.
The world is deprived
of Meyerhold.
How simple,
how devastatingly simple!

July 1994-March 1996

Lev Ozerov, trans. Boris Dralyuk

YURI OLESHA (1899-1960)

He yanked at his shirt collar,
ripping the cloth,
sending buttons flying.
"What on earth's the matter, Yuri Karlovich?"
No answer.
Just a flash—
no, a slash—
from under his brows.
Those eyes—gray to the point of blueness,
with a touch of the Black Sea's greenness
at evening time on the beach in Odessa.
The eyes of a sorcerer,
or of Vrubel's Pan,
who folds his mighty hands
but could have borne the earth
on his shoulders.
Yuri Olesha kept silent a long time,
and I too kept silent,
thinking of how to retreat,
to leave unnoticed.
A man sometimes needs
to be alone—
this is no less important
than a talk with a friend.
Finally, he began to pace
diagonally across the room,
stooping gravely,
one hand behind his back,
the other in the bosom of his torn shirt.
His eyes slashed
at me again.

Then he suddenly stopped
and stared—
not at me, but somewhere off in the distance.
"I offered one of the journals
a new novella, perhaps even a novel,
and read them a passage.
Can you guess what happened?"
A pause. "Were they interested?
Not for a minute!
'Give us *Envy*!' they said.
'*Envy*'s been written' I told them...
And you ask me 'What's the matter?'"
"'What's the matter?'" he repeated,
lifting his heavy chin
and coming closer,
very close, face-to-face.
Solemnly, distinctly, he pronounced:
"Please remember—Yuri Olesha
is an unwanted writer..."
And after a pause,
in a tone that was softer, more tired:
"I've earned the right to despair..."
and he again began to pace
diagonally across the room—
silently, sternly.
Now like a prisoner, or an exile,
like in that painting of Van Gogh's—
with the convicts moving in a circle
behind prison walls.
When he grew tired
of wrath and fury,
I persuaded him
to go out for a stroll.

He needed to let his mind wander,
as did I—
this storytelling wizard's
fortunate audience.
We step out of the gate
and see a van drive up
to Valentin Katayev's dacha
across the way.
Television technicians
come leaping out like paratroopers:
cameramen, directors, assistants,
assistants to the assistants,
electricians and observers.
People get tangled in wires,
stab tripods into the ground,
loudly survey the buildings—
weary townsfolk out in nature.
They visit two or three homes,
ignoring Olesha—
who has long ago fallen out of favor.
Into disgrace.
"Let's get out of here quick!"
Yuri Karlovich cried
and turned sharply to the left.
He marched down the alley,
at once hunched over
and throwing back his head,
as only he could.
He walked—he, who'd written *Envy*
but hadn't envied the rich.
He'd refused to sit on committees,
to give idle speeches
in the presence of bosses,
to join prestigious delegations;

he had turned his back
on many other seductions
for which others had fallen.
He became the Francois Villon
of the Soviet Middle Ages.
He found a beggar more appealing
than a plump latifundista.
Better no day without a line
than a room at an exclusive hotel.
He wrote for the drawer.
When I looked at other authors,
I recalled what they had published.
When I looked at Olesha,
I thought of what he hadn't.
And then, right at the moment
when that thought entered my head,
he again brought his face up close
to my face.
He gazed at me with those sorcerer's eyes,
gray to the point of blueness,
touched with the Black Sea's greenness,
and said: "Yuri Olesha—
an unwanted writer."
He articulated each word still more distinctly
than before.
Silently, we walked into the woods,
and silently walked out.
Twilight's veil
darkened.
Olesha said:
"I looked around,
and to tell you the truth, my friend,
I don't understand a goddamn blessed thing."

"Yury Karlovich, please!"
"Quiet! Don't even try
calming me down.
I specialize in agitation..."
When we came up to the gate
of the house where we were staying,
Olesha threw back his head distractedly:
"Look—what a starry sky!"
And he began to list the stars,
which he knew
intimately,
not only by surname,
but even by first name.

18 June, 1994

Rikudah Potash
Translated from the Yiddish by Michael Casper

ASHTORETH

Today I saw Ashtoreth—
Ashtoreth, with a mouth of white teeth.

She sold peaches
with red faces and a yellow shimmer,
and she herself
had a carved wooden neck
with a lot of silver medallions;
her plaits hung down
like two dark ear-locks.

And it was an Indian summer!
As I looked at her feet,
at her painted nails,
a hundred-year-long day glided out
on the sky
with a crooked white sail.

Rikudah Potash, trans. Michael Casper

LAST WILL AND TESTAMENT OF A YELLOWED LEAF

1.

The kingdom of leaves has
its own calendar,
its own notary,
its own house of law,
its own judge,
its own ruling.

As a leaf drops
in late fall,
and the wind goes to sleep
under the roof,
the rain rains out a prayer
for the whole leaf community.

2.

A leaf lies,
yellow,
quartered.
With yellow fingers
on the parchment sky
a leaf-will inscribes
letter after letter.
And windows cry
at someone's death.

David Samoylov
Translated from the Russian by Peter Oram

BEATRICE

They say that Beatrice was a city-dweller
a nasty woman, overweight and plain,
yet love had fallen onto stern old Dante
like a golden earring onto a stone.

He picked her out, long kept her in his sight,
then, gazing at her, took her by the hand
forever, singing songs in sweet delight
of this unsavoury Madonna that he'd found.

But she, despite her lack of education,
heard through the kitchen's din a secret call,
and, having recognized her own damnation,
she languidly put on a string of pearls.

And, humbly heeding presages of doom
she grew paler, prettier, lost weight,
her cheeks acquired a pallid, pinkish bloom
like cold, dead pearls against a body's heat.

He, basking in the glow of future ages,
complained she shirked responsibilities,
not knowing how she felt, condemned forever
to market haggling over groceries.

David Samoylov, trans. Peter Oram

Doors slammed and children screamed on undeterred,
the servants bustled, always in a hurry.
But they were two and didn't need a third,
this woman and her Dante Alighieri.

"WAS I REALLY HAPPY THEN…"

Was I really happy then,
in early youth, with my first love
when the world first drew me in
and hope was still a fledgling dove?

Oh, what a trance I lived in then …
the times when we two sat together
in the darkened cinema,
elbows pressed against each other…

but that first love was doomed forever,
for our each and every word,
however filled with dreams, however
sweet and tender, was absurd.

Somewhere around the middle of
the film, contrary to the plot
you drew your hand back to remove
it from my fingers, tense and hot.

The lights come on: one moment we
are sitting in their sterile glow,
the next we're wandering aimlessly
across a field of fallen snow.

And underneath your fiery copper
curls I see you blushing, see
the plentiful and ripening fruit
of catastrophic destiny…

David Samoylov, trans. Peter Oram

BEAUTY

She's like a fiddle at my shoulder, and
I press her to me like a fiddle player;
her hair streams down my shoulders, layer on layer
like music with no sound.

She's a fiddle at my shoulder, all the same
what can she ever know of song's elation
What can I know of her? What can the flame
know of the lamp? Or God of His creation?

Great talent, after all, is unaware:
of its own worth: still truer this must be
of beauty: she steps forward easily
and never tires in her desire to share.

She's like a fiddle at my shoulder, and
although her harmonies are complicated
we do not find them hard to understand:
we feel their pain, are never alienated.

And so we put aside all strife and care,
and as, in our illuminated moments,
we listen to her long, slow cantilenas
we recognize that high significance
that of itself's entirely unaware.

Vladimir Vysotsky
Translated from the Russian by
Yevgeniy Sokolovsky

FAREWELL

Ships shall rest for a while then, course-bound, depart
But they later return as the storms test their courage
I will also come back from my voyage to start
As a matter of course, as a matter of course, a new voyage.

All return in the end, save the greatest of friends,
Save the most dedicated and treasured of women
All return, but the ones who are most in demand,
I distrust both myself, I distrust both myself and the omens from heaven.

But I want to believe in a different trend—
That destroying one's ships never will be encouraged,
I will soon reappear with new projects and friends
I will soon sing again, I will soon sing again, celebrating my voyage.

1966

Vladimir Vysotsky, trans. Yevgeniy Sokolovsky

"I ALWAYS TREATED PHANTOMS WITH DISTRUST..."

I always treated phantoms with distrust,
I did not plan an Eden-bound transit,
The sea of lies gulped down the teaching caste
And spewed it out near Magadan in frenzy.

I did not differ from the lowbrow folk,
And even if I did, then very little,
I felt at ease when Budapest was mocked,
And Prague did not fragment my heart completely.

So we made lots of noise in life and theater:
Still a befuddled, immature pack!
But soon we would be recognized much better.
Who wants to challenge us?   Let's wring his neck!

Yet we identified despite our fervor
Bad omens long before the cold arrived .
Disgraceful apprehension would wash over
And wreck our souls with paralyzing fright.

And while the executions never crushed us
We too, displaying ever lowered eyes,
Were children of the dreadful years of Russia—
The stagnant age poured vodka into us.

1979

Anton Yakovlev

EVERGREEN

Make like a tree and wake the bears in March,
breakdancing in the sexy western wind.
Rain your small rain, but—Christ!—not on my head!

Make like a Christmas tree in Midland Park.
Bellow those chewed-up carols on your tape—
but don't forget I'd never play that shit.

Lose that spring chicken photograph of me
you used to stare at while you listened to
your favorite Brodsky poem on repeat.

Spare me the sap of your incessant praise—
your balsam fragrance smacks of tartar sauce
in oyster shacks along the Berlin Wall.

If ever I come back around New York,
stay planted like a cedar down the Shore,
don't run into my ass at *KGB*.

Don't send me videos of dogs you've trained,
your brush with death at Frank Sinatra's home,
your dueling bagpipes at *Blarney's Pub*.

Make like a tree and overrun the fields.
Crash unannounced into a laundromat
and bleach my halo out of your armpits.

Haven't I done enough to make you leave—
answered my phone while you confessed your love,
regifted your grandmother's wedding band?

Long-distance trucks sign off at exit ramps;
eyes roll; bone marrow moves from soul to soul;
staunch transvestites turn into chauvinists—

everything changes. Only you stand by,
left-field old faithful, salmon run of care,
Grizzly sequoia in a forest fire.

THE GIFT

Patched up with tape and webs,
a hole in the wall reveals
a dusty Nabokov novel inside the shed,
your birthday present to me when I turned 22.

When the walls of the shed are knocked down,
dead butterflies will land on its cover.

I'll save it, of course.
I'll put it in my top drawer.
When we're both old,
I'll bring it to you
and suggest we read it together,

though you'll only say, "No, I didn't
give this to you. You must be
thinking of someone else."

STILL LIFE

I

Happiness fell on you like a Christmas light
carelessly thrown onto a midtown tree.

Suddenly you were exactly in the right place,
living the life you couldn't afford to mess with.

Fireworks dashed all about your home.
Curtains blocked the distracting Sun.

Every night you kneeled in a smattering
of time-honored cinders, praying for stasis.

Once a hero of piano-bangers,
you fell to cautious diminuendos.

Emeritus of artful in-your-face,
you earned a Master's in backpedaling.

A neologism came to you in a dream.
You rubbed the back of your head until you forgot it.

II

No curtain lasts forever.
Stitches rot away, light reenters.

Boring cherry trees outside the window
confronted you with merciless maroon.

Everything you held to be your world
slid like ducklings down a duckling slide.

Happiness is nothing if nothing happens.
Staring at your own hands eventually blinds you.

III

You open your doors to let the fireworks out,
but they are merely cinders on your floor.

You try to return the lights to the Christmas tree,
but it's already September.

Stray dogs peek into your house
but find it too depressing to come in.

A high-speed ferry sounds like an angry geezer.
Someday you'll come downhill and stow away.

Until then, small birds build their nests,
but not in your hair.

THREE MEXICAN BORDER POETS

Martín Camps
Translated from the Spanish by Anthony Seidman

THE TOUGH DENIM OF THE SEA

I am awakened at dawn by the caterwaul
of a mermaid in the bay.
A voice reminding us
that the sea is still there,
beneath a thick blanket of fog.
The sea is a river that remains still,
and when we arise each morning, it will be there,
entirely blue, in order to give us a second chance.

José Eugenio Sánchez
Translated from the Spanish by Anthony Seidman and Ken Montenegro

I'D PROBABLY LEARN TO LOVE HER IF ONLY SHE'D SPRAY BOURBON ON HER BODY

she's just scrubbed her crotch with a towel
because she was pinned beneath some middle aged john
whom she forced to strap on a rubber
and she danced for him and sucked him off
for the hundred bucks they had haggled
on the corner of Sunset & Western

and now she adjusts her nylons & leather miniskirt
she puts on her high heels
zips up her black jacket leaving her bust partially exposed
she teases her hair
says goodbye and smiles before shutting the door
and beneath a persistent drizzle she walks
down a lit & abandoned street

she drags her handbag with a vague apathy
and there's a bit of poetry in this

César Silva Márquez
Translated from the Spanish by Anthony Seidman

CARNE ASADA

Last Saturday morning of each month,
it advances, an iceberg among the shoppers,
inviolate, nestled in a white basket,
down the supermarket aisles

five pounds of meat
kosher salt and beer

he bought unwrapped and grilled everything in April
straight to the flames in his garden
far from the traffic-jams
and the appointments hanging from telephone wires

he's got ribs and tenderloins and he dreams
of coals perfectly white-hot

his mind drifts far from turmoil

now he pictures the thin juice, the ribs, the bone's taste
the thin grease glistening on the tenderloins

it's the end of the month and hunger touches us
the salt slowly saturates the rib
now we listen to the meat's sizzle and the fluttering flags of fire

a hand clutches a beer
and the meat smells like centuries of bloodshed and hunting

SEVEN ROMANIAN POETS

Ion Vinea
Translated from the Romanian by
Georgiana Galateanu-Farnoaga and Boris Dralyuk

THE ROAD BACK

Neither today, nor tomorrow: the day of yesterday.
Where are the hours lost to the ages?
I miss the vanished gazes—
voices call me like ghosts
through timeless memory.

I want the blood of the sun drying on the lakes,
the bellow of buffaloes at twilight,
the rustling of the garden between walls,
the whiff of wax fruit in the winter pantries,
the camphor-scented penumbra of the reps-cloth drawing room
in mirrors filled with the waters of forgetting,
in which my brother, who has left the living,
lay between candles.

I want father's steps ascending the stairs,
the bronze gong announcing dinner,
I want to hear my name again, mother,
uttered softly and precisely
as it has lingered, floating, in the wasteland of my thoughts.

Ion Vinea, trans. Georgiana Galateanu-Farnoaga and Boris Dralyuk

I want to lock the spell in the house, an iron bar across the gate,
to trim the candle in the alcove,
and for my Priam to howl at the cold signs of the zodiac,
into the night, alone, in the dead zone,
feeling miserable, deserted,
when, in my lavender-scented bedding,
I fall asleep for eternity.

Tristan Tzara
Translated from the Romanian by
Georgiana Galateanu-Farnoaga and Boris Dralyuk

DEAR COUSIN, BOARDING-SCHOOL GIRL

Dear cousin, boarding-school girl, dressed in black, with a white collar,
I love you because you are simple and dream,
and you are good, you cry, and tear up letters that have no meaning,
and you are sad that you're far from your family, that you study
with the nuns, where it isn't warm at night.
Once again you count the days left before the break,
and you remember a Spanish engraving
where an *infanta* or duchess of Braganza
sits in her ample dress, like a butterfly on a corolla,
and amuses herself by feeding cats while awaiting her knight,
with parrots and other small animals on the rug—
birds that fell from the sky,
and, down by the armchair, which is in mourning,
a hound, slender and panting,
like an ermine stoal that has slid from her shoulders.
She wants to rise, but
she remembers, and strokes the necklace at her throat
because she glimpses the knight—and that's all:
Sister Beatrice or Evelina approaches the bench,
a teacher of history, or of Greek, or of Latin,
o, why do the days pass so slowly…
Leaves and flowers fall like pages from a calendar;
life is sad, but it's still a garden!

And the *infanta* or duchess of Braganza
is dozing off again, or losing her importance, because you are
    counting—
adding up on your fingers—the days left before the break

I start the letter again and write: Ma chère cousine
Je croyais hier entendre dans ma chambre ta voix tandre et câline.

1915

Ana Blandiana
Translated from the Romanian by
Georgiana Galateanu-Farnoaga and Boris Dralyuk

QUARANTINE

Pain is not contagious,
I assure you, pain cannot be transmitted.
No twisted nerve in my brother's body
Can trigger a twinge in mine.

Pain is not contagious, pain
Separates more atrociously than walls.
No quarantine isolates so perfectly.
What I say is banal—that's the point.

God, how much literature we contain!
Feelings—remember?—we learned about them in school.
They cry around the deathbed,
But none of them catches death.

Do not fear, keep altruistic vigils by the sick.
You won't catch their pain, don't worry.
He's dead. Does anyone want to follow him?
Only traditional dirges.

Oradea, 16/17 October 1964

Ion Caraion
Translated from the Romanian by
Georgiana Galateanu-Farnoaga and Boris Dralyuk

THE STRANGER IN THE WINDOW

I was returning from my own burial.
I had been asked to talk about myself.
But I forgot where and I forgot who
came out of the graveyard with a hospice on his back.

Clusters of flames. The smoke of spring.
The specters of houses glued to the asphalt.
Inquisition—Middle Ages—the heat—
the sun unraveling… bells tolling… night falling…

At dusk the Dusseldorf girls sang cheerfully.
They sang even when speaking.
And they came, and they went,
amorphous twilights in amorphous air.

While the cities… the cities had flaxen hair.
I walked past you, Lord, as past a deserted wall.
The era is so tired!
People grow old from home to the tram stop.

The fins of carp or the mustaches of catfish
will make their bed again.
We gambled. We lost.
Don't interrupt the games, gentlemen!

Ion Caraion, trans. Georgiana Galateanu-Farnoaga and Boris Dralyuk

Clad in eagles, in myth and minerals
(but I forgot where and I forgot who…)
I was approached by
the stranger in the window, the moon, or myself.

1969

Ileana Mălăncioiu
Translated from the Romanian by
Georgiana Galateanu-Farnoaga and Boris Dralyuk

MY SISTER, THE EMPRESS

My sister, the empress,
got upset with us,
took her crowns and left,
but mother and father think
she will come back.

Surely she'll come back, father says,
how can you pass
from one kingdom to another
in your slippers.

But mother has a woman's soul,
she feels her daughter can't return
wearing a crown and slippers
in broad daylight.

She'll come back at night, says mother,
she'll come back tomorrow, says father,
I alone know that my sister is gone
and that's that.

I saw the road she walked down
littered with her seven crowns
to disguise it from our parents
and I came across the tracks of her slippers
in the other kingdom.

Mariana Marin
Translated from the Romanian by
Georgiana Galateanu-Farnoaga and Boris Dralyuk

ELEGY

Lord,
if only I could rest at a mountain sanatorium
among pink and blue and pills,
a sanatorium with a strong scent of fir trees
and soft carpeting,
with stylish ladies, driven to neurosis
by small, pleasant, conjugal conflicts.
If only I could have a trauma like measles,
the pattering of summer rain,
a neurosis like silk,
after which you are loved even more:
a neurosis like chamomile vapor,
after which you're even more confused,
celestial,
after which the flow of your femininity assaults the world,
heals it, gives it the frisson of a treasure only you know.
If I could rest in any life scenario,
in various simple, honest out-of-the-way corners,
where there is only a bed for sleeping
and a basin for me to vomit
all that you took from me, Lord, by the way you grant your gifts,

and keep vomiting.

1999

Florin Iaru
Translated from the Romanian by
Georgiana Galateanu-Farnoaga and Boris Dralyuk

I Saw Everything

I saw Kennedy's
burial
broadcast via Telstar,
the first telecommunication
satellite
permitted under socialism.

I saw Ceauşescu
on the balcony,
mesmerizing the crowds
one August morning.
I saw the moon in the palm of my hand,
and Armstrong,
walking away from the lander
like a weightless drunk.
I saw Nadia.
She had just gotten her first score
of ten
in her life.
Then I saw the Romanian
revolution live,
and I felt I was breaking
the black-and-white screen
with the last gasp of youth.

Florin Iaru, trans. Georgiana Galateanu-Farnoaga and Boris Dralyuk

I've seen nothing since.
Is Telstar still up there?
Or did it fall?

It fell.
May it rest in peace!

2014

Essays

MOTHER-TONGUE MATTERS

Maria Jastrzębska

The photographs of my childhood are black-and-white. Not only the pictures but the values seemed more fixed then. We Poles were the good guys, Russians were bad and so on. Like wildflowers springing up between cracks of concrete, I began to notice things which didn't fit this scheme. My favourite grandmother spoke Polish with an accent. The grown-ups' talk of occupation and atrocities was the backdrop to my childhood. But in a child's way I was also concerned with my own—tomboyish—pursuits.

Babcia Zaza Went to Paris

Sssh!—it's a secret
who Babcia Zaza is.
That's why she speaks more softly
than anyone else I know.
Her vowels are wrapped in silk
and rabbit fur. They kneel down
in front of all the consonants
that stamp their feet and blow
into their hands like soldiers.

Soldiers cut open my other Babcia—
Lilka's—throat after they'd ----- her.

Babcia Zaza never swears.
Speaks French as well as Polish,
wears ruby rings and puts on airs.
She travelled by train all the way
to Paris! Brought me back a doll —
not like the others with blue eyes,
blonde ponytails, chiffon petticoats
I'd never wear—this one
has green eyes and a boy's short hair!

It turned out my grandmother was actually Russian, not Polish. Years later in Warsaw I discovered a whole branch of our family who was half-Jewish. No one had told me about these things. A different and more complicated picture had to be pieced together.

All children, in a sense, grow up in a country different from that of their parents. We moved from Warsaw to London in the late '50s. The Iron Curtain made it an irrevocable move with no to and froing. I soon rebelled against my family and community but like every immigrant child I was the interpreter, mediating between my parents and the institutions and authorities of our new country.

While English children were out playing, teachers at the Polish Saturday school I resentfully attended did their best to win us over with the elegies of Jan Kochanowski or the dates of famous Polish battles. What I did learn was how hard people had fought to preserve our language, and that teachers had risked (and lost) their lives to teach Polish language and literature under Nazi occupation.

In English school I learned nothing of Polish history or European literature. I went from Walter de la Mare to Ted Hughes and A. E. Houseman. Found Yevtushenko (thanks to Penguin Modern European Poets) and Sylvia Plath. My first encounters with Zbigniew Herbert (thanks again to PMEP) and Mrożek (thanks to the local theatre) were in English.

Later I found more contemporary Polish writers, almost always in translation. It was through them and through visiting Poland, once it became possible again, that I began to build my own Poland, distinct from the émigré one, though inevitably the immense, never fully expressed grief and nostalgia of my parents' generation burst through, a river flooding the plain. Its force, like the after-effects of any war or occupation, not confined to the generation who had lived through it. I still find myself writing about 'their' war, time and time again.

Wooden Bird

What about the soldiers? What of them?
When the later ones came, how did they seem to you?
They were grown-ups. I don't know.
They had rabbit fur ushankas and heavy coats.
Yes, they sat in the square. *That's it?*
They wanted bread.
Did you give them any? My mother gave me some
to hand them.
       They were carving birds.
Out of lime wood, I think, because it's softer.
I gave one of the soldiers some bread
in return for a wooden bird.
I used to run with it, my arm stretched
high above my head.
One of its wings broke off.
But all through the war, through grey sky,
over blue oceans, over green lakes and rivers,
red dots of capital cities, brown bumps
of the mountains around and around
       the astonishing globe we flew together.

Trying to escape my family, yet ill at ease in English society, I felt increasingly isolated and 'sick of' explaining everything 'to everybody'. I was battling pride in my culture with English embarrassment. Polish people speak more loudly—to this day if English friends hear me speaking Polish they think I'm having an argument. My mother complained if the grocer tried to sell her tomatoes which were too soft.

I'd cringe in full teenage fashion. Luckily, I discovered Black American writers—the only ones who made sense to me. I fell on anthologies like *This Bridge Called My Back—Writings by Radical Women of Color,* hungry for every word. Eventually I also found the writer Ewa Hoffman, a Polish Jew who had left Poland in the same year as us and who articulated the sense of longing, of *tęsknota* and *żal,* the dislocation and the cross-cultural generation gap.

Par Avion

When I send your parcel, there's always
a queue. I've forgotten the cellotape,
so I have to buy more as well as a *flat pak.*
I want to take off my coat, but there's nowhere
to put it and I'm already carrying too much:
your presents, my hat, gloves and now the box.

Luckily Rena takes pity on me, shows me
how to undo the flaps. I'm still trying
to join them all together, when an old woman
stands next to me. In a brown fake fur coat
and flesh-coloured tights, she's bent
almost double, filling in a form.

Ripping cellotape with my teeth, I smile
and make room for her. Silently she points
to everything I keep dropping. Does Antoś
even *like* Spiderman, will Paweł think
a rucksack's boring, maybe Ewka would have
preferred pink instead of lime green?

It used to be simpler: you could send
Nescafe, tea or, since it was still rationed,
always more chocolate. Before that
people sent blankets, men's jackets, Ceres fats
no one there knew what to do with. Or else
it was Odorono and injections of liver extract.

It's not as if we're the first exchanging gifts
across this divide; before us our mothers
and grandmothers worrying if they'd sent
the right thing, would it arrive in one piece,
like the bottle of halibut oil, which did,
the 'heavenly' blue dress, exactly the right size.

Babcie over there sent me classics, favourites
in hardback no one here had heard of:
Tuwim, Sienkiewicz, Słowacki. Orphan
Marysia or the billy goat forever in trouble
and Hałabała who lived in a tree hollow,
frying bilberry pancakes on a tiny wood-stove.
Are *you* worrying what to send us? Please,
no more stuffed birds. No matter how colourful.
But send pictures—of anything, people
on a tram. In my photo of Ewka she's still
a toddler, but probably by now she's a Goth.
Would she have preferred something black?

By the time I've stuck everything down,
the old woman is leaving. 'Cheerio!' I call
after her, but she can't hear me. I reach the front
of the queue, place your parcel on the scales at last.
I've stuffed the empty spaces with today's
sports page, which I normally use as kindling.

But will the cellotape keep your parcel
safe, all that way, crammed into holds,
crossing borders through thick snow to arrive
in a quiet dawn at your door? I wish
I'd bought the thicker kind. Rena says:
Best to send this as small packet.

I went to school and university in the UK. As I grew older my
mother-tongue receded into the subject matter of family conversation
and domesticity. It became harder to argue about -isms, to talk politics
and art. I was learning new forms of discourse—academic, professional,
political, feminist, personal, sexual. It was the '60s, then the '70s. We
were a generation convinced we could change the world. My mother
cursed 'angielski relatywizm' whereas I—seeing in it possibilities for
liberation and tolerance—embraced it. My role as interpreter also
meant trying to translate *back* to my family the excitement of what I
was discovering, but this proved so difficult that, at times, I gave up
trying.

Grandfather Clock

Have you seen this? your mother cries
and you know it's not an obituary
(though obituaries are what she checks
each day) nor an article reprimanding
the communist regime. Right there
on the grainy page it's Basia—
Basia Żarek—standing under a banner that says
Campaign for Homosexual Equality.
How did the Polish—and Soldier's—
Daily get a photograph like that?
She didn't, wouldn't, couldn't have
sent it in herself.

The solemn grandfather clock
is beating out the hour. A recent arrival
along with blue crockery and the roses
your mother dug up from your grandparents'
dismantled house and garden.
What, she says, *is a Polish girl doing
with all those pederasts?*
I don't know, you say, *we're not really
in touch.* The clock stops striking.
I'm off then, you close the door as quickly,
as quietly as you can.

Last year I was invited to be animateur at Fabrica Gallery in Brighton, where I now live. I worked alongside *I See Infinite Distance Between Any Point and Another*—an intimate film portrait by The Otolith Group of incredible poet, painter, and philosopher Etel Adnan reading extracts from her poem "The Sea." I called my project *unquietborder* and focused on the notion of us all crossing borders. Adnan herself was born in Beirut and moves between many languages, including Greek, Arabic, French and English. I explored what happens when we cross a border. What's spoken about, what's kept quiet?

As part of my enquiry I asked the public to interact with me by responding to 3 questions, beloved of U.K. immigration authorities: Where do you come from? What's the purpose of your visit? Do you have anything to declare? They wrote in and told me how they had 'arrived':

without so much as a second glance, through tunnels, out of semi-detached existence, night-time, convention, make-believe, from watching *Kinetica Bloco*, the edge of the world, heaven, a sea of memories, earth, sun, a crowd of women, from inside, from mothers, climates where crickets sing night and day, evasive fathers, the past, the unknown, a puzzle, straight off a roller coaster ride...

They declared:

that they were carrying songs, sonnets, childhood
baggage, a racist education, suitcases of doubts and fear,
without looking where they were going; they invoked
green, imprints, secrets, hair colour, a trillion cells, love,
language, lust, kindness, confusion, alcoholic parents,
passion, truth, uncertainty...

Their purpose:

to gaze at the nape of a neck, to grow vegetables, to
listen, struggling between the place they were from and
where they lived, to love the Third Quartet, to grow old,
to be free, to disagree, to travel light, crossing borders of
hesitation, through the Green Zone, looking for a way
out...

Such responses surpassed my expectations. People got it. They
grasped that we are all moving between cultures—not just those of us
who are foreigners.

Recently, I gave a reading at an event called "Migration Stories—
Can Home Be Translated?" along with the Ghanaian writer Nii
Ayikwei Parkes and Peruvian poet Sophia Buchuk at the Free Word
Centre in London.

This event too was about crossing borders and, more specifically,
the language we need to do that. Introducing us, the writer Carole
Angiers began by speaking about loss—the inevitable loss incurred
through exile or migration. I found my inner teenager rebelling once
more against that inevitability, and yet a sense of loss has shaped
everything I write. Are we mourning or celebrating? Or both at once?

Sophia Buchuk spoke of celebrating the culture, its customs and
ancestors left behind. Nii Ayikwei Parkes spoke of the gift of having
grown up in an African society where people spoke so many different
languages you couldn't possibly know them all. It taught him to look
beyond words when communicating with others.

Arguments about translating poetry are often polarised between fidelity to the original and the re-imagining of a text—a dichotomy I have never been comfortable with. This dichotomy has been questioned, more ably than I could manage, by poets like D. M. Black, who debunks the view that we should make only 'versions', since translation is so unsuccessful.

What is clear, however, is that translation often *feels* impossible. This is the case whether we are translating from another language or translating ourselves, our own memories and experiences, as all writers do. And like many writers I have a love-hate relationship with language.

Ollie Brock, translator-in-residence at *Free Word*, collected 'untranslatable words' prior to our event, and there was a lively discussion of which concepts people struggle most to get across, such as the Portuguese word *saudade,* which translates more easily into Polish than English. (www.FreeWordOnline.com/content/2013/02/audio-untranslatable-words/) But it is this very impossibility which provides us with the creative spark. We are not recording machines. Communication involves an act of transformation. All poetry is an art of the impossible, and for poets it is the impossible which thrills and challenges.

In my work I occasionally introduce a Polish word or phrase, not so much because it's something untranslatable, but simply to give a flavour of the language. An integral aspect of any culture is its food. In this poem I list some favourites:

Polski Sklep

When he opened the doors, smells of kabanos,
new greens, rye bread and honey cake reached us

from somewhere I could only just remember, a place
our mothers talked about.

Every Wednesday we heard the van's horn
as it stopped in the middle of our street.

If English neighbours watched through net curtains
as we dashed out, we didn't care.

All of us—*Pani Bogusia* who said I spoke beautifully
until her daughter told her I'd called her a monkey

and *Pani Iwonka* with peroxide hair who tripped out
in a dressing gown—*No jak tak można?!*—pushed

to the front of the queue, string bags open. I'd be close
behind Mama, tugging her arm. *Halva, buy us halva!*

The *Panie* flirted, bartering with the driver—a smiling man,
sweaty under his thick moustache.

My proud Mama, coral lips pressed together, wouldn't
stoop to that, but when he paid her compliments,

cajoling her to buy that extra portion of his best yeast cake,
fresh herring, she shook her head and then

let out a sigh, breathing again.

Why, asked our interviewer at the Free Word event, did I 'bother'
writing about my Polish upbringing and community when that was
surely all in the past, as I have moved away into an English-speaking
environment and write in English? "How can you not write about
childhood", I spluttered. Every writer does. Why would I turn my
back on the riches of a bi-cultural upbringing? It is the diversity of
cultures and languages which makes living in Britain not only bearable,
but engaging.

Herring

No one but him is left who'd remember
the stench, when one of us—nobody owned up—
knocked over the bucket of herrings curing
for Wigilia. Or our mother's curses: *pig's blood,*
pig's bone, I told them to mind as she scrubbed
the flagstones, the fishes' wide open eyes
as she thrashed about the cramped space,
their gaze like that of the glass-eyed fish surprised
by a hook in our great-uncle's painting.
She detested it but, out of love for our father,
hung it in pride of place beside the loud clock.
Was that a herring too or pike? Silvery green or striped?
Another fish out of water—salt, sweet? It hardly matters now.
We haven't spoken in years, but he'd know.

Writing about the past is problematic and I am concerned in my
work not only with how we deal with it individually but also collectively.

The Jackal Is Considered by the Meeting

The Curator sighs: the same arguments every time.
The lobby who say the public needs
enticing in, not more recollections of ill-treatment.
        So in fact a side-striped jackal cub,
even though it bit and scratched a little, seems ideal.
Children would love it. They would want
to pet it just as Verusha Grigorova's five children did.
No one knows where they found it.
Or knows which streets in Tbilisi they wandered through
on their way home from school. (Afterwards
they said it had been sunning itself behind
the Russian barber's, asleep on a heap of rubble.)

Only that they brought it home and hid it in the yard
feeding it portions of their *khachapuri*, till one day
sweeping out the corners their mother screamed—
she'd found it tied to the apricot tree with a pyjama cord—
dropped her broom. The cub whimpered and she wailed:
Holy Mother of God, what have they done this time?
I'm forced to take lodgers and iron men's chemises.
How am I to feed my children?
Let alone this wild animal? They begged her
in all the languages they knew, in their native Polish—
in best schoolbook French, in Georgian, Russian—
to let them keep it and here the memory fades
and what we know is that as adults two were imprisoned,
two shot and the middle child, despite being released,
quickly developed consumption. All five of them
dead within ten to fifteen years even though
when the revolution came—sisters and brothers—
they'd found themselves on opposite sides
at a time when it's said jackals and people fought
for meat left on the bodies lying on every street.

My friend Louise Halvardsson wrote her first novel in Swedish, her second in English. Now, she told me recently, she has gone back to writing in Swedish and finds she writes more quickly and naturally. I couldn't do that, I said.

I am more at home in my adoptive mother-tongue. English has become my dominant language and I positively delight in it at every turn. Yet that is never the whole story. Polish—something 'other'—is never far away.

Ever since I can remember I wanted to write—even before I had learned how to. I carried a small 'book' with me everywhere. I'd like to think my poetry springs from that small bundle of folded papers full of illiterate squiggles in some muddle of my two languages.

One of the best ways I know of freeing up the mind for creativity is walking. Nowadays, I am more familiar with the old flint-stone sheep paths on the Sussex Downs, where gorse and chalk battle for space, than with the Alpine slopes of the Tatry Mountains, the lakes or primaeval forests of my own motherland. But no matter how rusty it gets, no matter how clumsy it feels, my mother-tongue is always there, in the subconscious, in half-remembered names of people and places, expressions or fragments of song. It is, as Guyanese British poet Grace Nichols says, 'the old one/ [from which] a new one has sprung'.

I have come full circle from the days of interpreting for my own family. In addition to teaching creative writing I work as a community interpreter. When I talk to young people arriving in the U.K. from Poland they are by no means certain as to whether England will prove a temporary home or an enduring one. For some of their children English too will become dominant; others will balance both languages. Recently one of my clients, a builder who has lived here for eight years, a man I wouldn't expect to talk of visiting therapists, put it to me like this: 'If I went back now I'd have to see a psychologist. I just wouldn't be able to adapt.' What was it he would have to readjust to, I asked him. 'Everything' he said, 'everything, the buses, the doctors, the supermarket, everything'. Everything, I thought, what an excellent topic for poetry.

NOTES

D. M. Black. "Faithful or Free Approaches to Translation." *Poetry London* 69 (Summer 2011).

Eva Hoffman. *Lost in Translation*. Vintage, 1989.

Cherrie Moraga and Gloria Anzaldua, eds. *This Bridge Called My Back—Writings by Radical Women of Color*. New York: Kitchen Table: Women of Color Press, 1983. Title poem by Donna Kate Rushin.

Grace Nichols. *The Fat Black Woman's Poems*. Virago, 1984.

"Babcia Zaza Went to Paris," "Grandfather Clock," "Herring," "Wooden Bird," "The Jackal Is Considered by the Meeting" were published in *At The Library of Memories* (Waterloo Press, 2013), "Par Avion" in *Everyday Angels* (Waterloo Press, 2009) © Maria Jastrzębska

MAMA RA

Azary Messerer

She appeared in films under the name of Ra Messerer. In the family she was often called Ra, and I knew this name long before I learnt of the ancient God of the Sun in Egypt. She had in fact been like the sun, radiating kindness and wisdom to all those around her.

Rakhil was born on March 4, 1902 , in Vilna, the largest center of Jewish culture at the time. Jews comprised 51% per cent of its population. But Rakhil could not remember Vilna (now Vilnius), because her family moved to Moscow when she was only two years old. Quoting her mother, Ra told me that among her ancestors on the maternal line there were Vilna's "tzadiks"—sages and healers. Since her mother's name was Shabad, perhaps relating to Tsemakh Chabad (1864-1935), a physician and a major public figure of Vilna. In the Jewish Encyclopaedia, I read that he was the prototype of the famous Dr. Doolittle. What a pity that I did not ask Kornei Chukovsky (who wrote Dr. Doolittle's Russian version) about this when I was lucky enough to have interviewed him in the late 60's in Peredelkino.

Apparently, Rakhil showed great ability in childhood, and despite the limitations imposed on the Jews she was admitted to the prestigious Moscow classic school founded by the Duchess of Lviv. Director of the school was her daughter, the Princess of Lviv and it was said that the girls "learn from the princes and the princesses." As a girl Rakhil loved music lessons most of all—she sang in the school choir—and she also liked to study the Russian language. Her Russian language teacher was a former populist[1], who had been imprisoned for some time for his

1   Member of a 19th Century socialist movement in Russia who believed that political propaganda among the peasantry would lead to the awakening of the masses and, through their influence, to the liberalization of the Tsarist regime.

revolutionary activities. He gave her only the perfect score for grammar and speech at school. I have met only a few people in my life with such a perfect command of Russian language. Most of them studied before the revolution in private schools, and Rakhil was one of them.

Alas, the sound film was invented after Rakhil's cinematic career had ended. Where many actresses were forced to leave the profession because of poor speech, her speaking abilities would have kept her in good stead.

Her education at school was interrupted by the Revolution of 1917. These were the hungry, cold years, and Rakhil at a very tender age had to help her mother take care of her younger sisters and brothers. Rakhil's younger sister Elizabeth (who also became an actress) wrote in her diaries:

"In our family Ra enjoyed great prestige as an elder sister and mother's 'Assistant Principal'. I remember that when I was little she combed my hair, took me out for walks and, when we visited friends, I would look up to her and wait for her nod of approval before asking for something. After our mother's early death she became like a mother for our youngest brother Alexander, who at the time was only 13 years old (Rakhil was 27)." At present Alexander has remained "the last of the Mohicans" in the Messerer family at the age of 93 and has teenage great grandchildren.

Rakhil often made important decisions that determined the fate of her siblings. For example, she was the only one in the family who knew about Asaf's passionate desire to study ballet. He was afraid to speak about his plans with his father, knowing that, for all his love for the theater, he would not approve of such a decision. Rakhil said to Osia (as she called Asaf), "if you love ballet so much, then you should study it." Asaf enrolled in a private ballet school at 16 years of age and achieved such phenomenal success that within two years he was admitted to the Bolshoi Theater's graduation class. This is when Rakhil decided that her younger sister Sulamith had all the inclinations to follow in the footsteps of her brother Asaf. She took Mita, as she was called in the family, to take entrance examination at the Choreographic School and even made her a pretty tutu. So both renowned artists chose ballet as a life career, partly thanks to Rakhil.

Rakhil was well aware of her siblings' creativity; they would often give home performances staged by their elder brother Azary , who later became a famous actor and director. Rakhil herself also played an active role in these performances and decided early to devote herself to art.

At nineteen, Rakhil was admitted to the Institute of Cinematography shortly after its foundation. During the entrance exam, the chairman of the examinations committee, Lev Kuleshov , asked her to perform a sketch—to catch a butterfly. Rakhil for a long time was creeping up to imaginary butterflies with the imaginary scoop net, failing to catch them. In the end, she started to cry with vexation so convincingly that the examiners themselves were almost in tears.

Along with Lev Kuleshov, she studied under such renowned directors and teachers as Jacob Protazanov and Dziga Vertov. Among her classmates there were future celebrity filmmakers like Ivan Pyrjev, Boris Barnet, and Vera Maretskaya , with whom she developed a long-term friendship. Students of VGIK gathered in the house of the Messerers, and had dancing parties with charades and masquerades. A soulmate of the company in her student years was her classmate Vladimir Plisetski—a witty, charming athlete. She met him at equestrian lessons. An excellent rider, he helped her master this skill important for a film actress.

At one of the parties he had brought along his older brother Mikhail. It so happened that both brothers were infatuated with beautiful Rakhil—it was a love triangle. But it was Mikhail who would eventually win her heart, and they got married. Eventually, Vladimir left the cinema, became a gymnast, an acrobat and an entertainer; he performed in Claudia Shulzhenko's show. During the war, he joined the front as a volunteer, heroically distinguished himself as a scout, having been dropped many times behind the front line with a parachute. Vladimir died in December 1941, during one of these desperately daring operations.

Rakhil's career could be called an overnight success. The great director Protazanov thought she was an exotic, biblical-type beauty (huge, sad eyes, raven black hair, and dark complexion) and gave her starring roles filmed in the new studio Uzbekfilm, which opened in

Tashkent. There, she co-starred in the movies "Second wife" (1927), "Leprous" (1928), "The Valley of Tears" (1929) and others. These films were a great success, and Rakhil's sad eyes stared off posters in many cinemas throughout the country. She played tragic heroines. Today, these films are still relevant, as their main theme was the liberation of women of the East from the yoke of Muslim Sharia law. For example, in the beginning of the film "The Second wife", Ra appears veiled— humble, downtrodden; by the end of the film, having experienced many disasters, she decides to revolt against the unhappy marriage and cruel relatives. These days, watching on TV women of Iran and Afghanistan, fighting for their rights, I am often reminded of Ra in her films shot in Uzbekistan.

There is no doubt that Rakhil was a talented actress; she was able to reach and touch her audience. And I find these movies particularly painful, because I know that Rakhil's life poised many severe tests for her, not unlike the lives of the heroines she played.

Apart from Tashkent, she worked on films set in the Altai mountains, in Kalmykia and in Kiev, where she starred in the film *The Daughter of a Rabbi*. It should be noted there were no stuntmen used in films at that time and actors had to do all the tricks themselves. Having already mastered the art of horse-riding, Rakhil now learned how to ride a motorcycle. In general, she was remarkably multi-skilled: staging plays, dancing, and, most importantly, taking bold decisions. Her courage and resourcefulness would help her survive the most testing trials in her life.

In 1925, Rakhil gave birth to a daughter, Maya. Rakhil continued to act in films in Tashkent and in Moscow, at the Mosfilm Studios. Occasionally, she brought Maya on set. Four-year-old Maya attended the premiere of the movie *Leprous*. During the film's climax, the heroine is thrown under the horse's hooves by bassmachis. Maya was in hysterics. Rakhil tried desperately to calm her down, saying that it was just a movie and not a real life. Yet Maya kept screaming, "But, Mommy, they killed you! They killed you!"

With the birth of the second child Alexander, Rakhil was forced to leave the cinema. Her husband was appointed manager of mines

Arktikugol and Consul of the USSR in the Norwegian arctic island of Spitsbergen, where he managed the production of coal. There were numerous articles written about this project including a book by the prominent poet-futurist Vadim Shershenevich. This book describes dramatic events: ships breaking through the ice and weathering severe storms on their way to Spitsbergen (located at 78 degrees north latitude). A steamer "Malygin" was squeezed by the blocks of ice, while a ship "Ruslan" got covered by ice and sank, with only a few on board managing to escape. Miners worked under dangerous conditions in permafrost, in continuing darkness.

In 1932, Rakhil arrived at Svalbard[2] with her baby Alik and a seven-year-old Maya on the last departing ship: they endured monstrous gales and storms, as all transportation was cut off for the next six months. It was soon revealed that Arktikugol, the organization responsible for the welfare of the workers and the polar explorers in Svalbard, had failed to deliver blankets. Rakhil, together with some other wives of miners, began to sew quilts from materials available in storerooms, deciding not to wait for the next delivery that would take six more months.

She worked as a telephone operator. But her time there was marked by her ability to bring some joy and laughter into the lives of the Soviet Arctic colony workers. She organized amateur concerts. Under her direction, an opera was staged, *The Little Mermaid,* where Maya played the role of the mermaid. Those in the audience could not have guessed that they were witnessing the debut of one of the greatest Russian performers of all time--The Prima Ballerina, Maya Plisetskaya. The family would often remember Pushkin's phrase that she uttered with naivete of a child: "And what is money, I do not know."

75 years later, Rakhil's younger son Azari (who became a well-known ballet teacher and choreographer) visited Spitsbergen. In the museum of Barentsburg he saw photos of his father and banknotes issued for internal use in Svalbard with the facsimile signature of his father, M. E. Plisetski. These are now a numismatic rarity. Azari added

2   Svalbard is an archipelago in the Arctic Ocean north of mainland Europe, about midway between mainland Norway and the North Pole.

to the museum's collection an inscribed miner's lamp, donated to his father by the miners of Barentsburg.

Rakhil, having returned back from the Arctic, led a relatively peaceful life for about two years. Mikhail Plisetsky was awarded medals and honors for his work, among them, an "Emka," car, one of the first Soviet made cars. Academician Otto Schmidt, who headed the General Directorate of the Northern Sea Route, appointed him as a general manager of the trust "Arktikugol, " and they were also given an apartment in the centre of Moscow. This was the height of the "good life" and bestowed official prestige on the family.

One remarkable event took place in January 1935: a special performance organized by the Messerer family. On that day actors and theatergoers crowded at the entrance of the MKHAT 2 theatre. The tumult was so great that the ushers had to stand outside the front doors in order to allow entry only to those with invitations.

The famous Messerer Five was comprised of three sisters and two brothers. The show included excerpts from the films in which Rakhil starred. Sulamith and Asaf performed the pas de deux from "Don Quixote" and their best solo. Azary and Elizabeth played scenes from several classic and contemporary plays and performed parodies on Stanislavsky, Nemirovich-Danchenko, Alisa Koonen, and others. The evening proved to be an enormous success.

But the fearful atmosphere in Moscow had already started to manifest itself, and the so-called Great Terror, unleashed by Stalin, soon was in force. Rakhil's husband Mikhail was arrested on April 30, 1937, when Rakhil was seven months pregnant. In her autobiography, Maya Plisetskaya describes in detail the scene of the arrest. Maya was then 11-years-old, and she was told that her father was "urgently summoned back" to Spitsbergen.

Later, Maya told me how she vividly remembered her father's hands, his long thin fingers with a scar from the sword fight (he had fought in the Civil War on the side of the Reds). She paused, then added that every day she sees in her mind's eye how they broke her father's hands... I could not believe her and asked, "Do you really mean every day?" "Yes, and often at night," she replied. I thought later that such powerful emotions must have been channelled into her work as a great ballerina and a tragic actress.

For Stalin and his henchmen it was not difficult to concoct a reason for the arrest and to eliminate any person, no matter how famous or well-regarded by the state in the past. Maya was not correct, writing that the reason for her father's arrest was the visit in 1934 to the USSR of his older brother , Lester Plesent, who had immigrated to America before World War I. Half a century after his arrest, in 1992-93 to be exact, Alexander, Rakhil's younger brother, gained access to the records of the interrogations of Mikhail Plisetsky. In the dossier No. 13060 (consisting of 12 volumes) the name of his American brother never appeared. But other reasons concocted by the investigators stand very clear from the yellowish pages: he was too loyal to his close friends when they experienced hard times. In Svalbard, Michael hired R.V. Pickel , who was considered to be officially in disgrace for his close links to the "deviationist" Zinoviev. Later, in 1936, Pickel "made a confession" at the famous public mock trial of Zinoviev, Kamenev and others. In particular, he acknowledged his "participation in an assassination attempt on Stalin's life." Soon after the trial he was shot and all those associated with him were also arrested. Michail Plisetsky rejected the monstrous accusations made against him for a long time, but in mid-July, unexpectedly, he signed a confession. And there was a reason for this incredible act: on July 13, 1937, Rakhil gave birth to Azari. On July 22, Rakhil returned with him home from the hospital. And on July 23 there was a telephone call and a voice on the other side said, "Do not ask who is calling but tell us—who was born?" Rakhil, frightened out of her wits, replied, "A boy."

That dreadful call was most likely made from the dungeon where Michael Plisetsky was being interrogated. The interrogators would use anything personal information or of emotional nature to squeeze a confession from the victims. Soon after they began to arrest "wives of the enemies of the people." In the early spring of 1938, Rakhil and baby Azari were taken away and later shipped to a labour camp.

On that day, Rakhil bought some flowers and was about to go out with children to see the ballet "Sleeping Beauty" at the Bolshoi, with

Asaf and Sulamith in the lead roles. When the secret police came for her, she told Maya to go with Alik by themselves, to give the flowers to Mita and Asaf and tell them that she was urgently "summoned to her husband to Spitsbergen" together with the baby.

Even before the performance had started, Sulamith learned that the children came to the 16th official entrance by themselves. She wrote in her memoir: "I do not remember how I danced; I recall only my brother whispering in my ear 'Keep dancing, keep dancing, maybe nothing bad has happened…'"

During the intermission Mita called Rakhil. Her terrible fears were confirmed: Rakhil and little Azari were arrested. Sulamith took Maya to live with her, and Asaf took Alik who was a year older than his own son Boris.

Rakhil was jailed in a cavernous circular cell in the notorious Butyrskaya prison along with dozens of other mothers, many with screaming babies. Inmates would try their best to support each other morally. They would sing a lullaby in the Butyrskaya that Rakhil would later recall:

Early in the morning, at dawn,

Come the guards.

The children stand roll-call.

The sun would rise.
A thin ray
On a moist wall,

And touch the tiny prisoner,
Someone's dearest.
But the gloomy abode

Will not brighten.
Who will return the rosy cheeks
To my little sun?
Behind bars and locks
Days last a year.
Children cry and even mothers

Cry sometimes.

But the new generation is nurtured,

With hearts like steel;
My child, never believe

Your father was a traitor.

The last lines sound a discordant note to the dark lyricism of the poem. However, they reflect Rakhil's credo. She was a frail little woman, but with the strength of character not unlike a hardened soldier. Her investigators soon realized that she was a hard nut to crack. She did not make any compromises and denied that she knew anything about the alleged "crime" of her husband. In her case it was recorded "she denies everything, but most probably she knew all about it".

After Butyrskaya prison Rakhil and Azari were sent to the Gulag or rather to the so-called "Algeria"—Russian acronym for Akmolinskiy Camp for the wives of traitors. They were transported in cattle cars packed with political prisoners and ordinary criminals. Rakhil learnt from a gypsy woman who slept with one of the guards that they were being taken to Kazakhstan. Cold winds whistled through the cracks in the walls of the carriages. The prisoners suffered from terrible thirst, as they were fed salty dried fish without water to drink. But even more she was tormented by the thought of not being able to let her close ones know about her whereabouts. To remedy this, she had put to use something she learnt from jailbirds.

On a piece of paper Rakhil wrote a few lines with matches: "We're moving in the direction of Karaganda, to the camp in the Akmolinsky region. The child is with me..." She also wrote down her family's address in Moscow: "Dzerzhinsky Str., Building 23, Apt. 3". Rakhil folded the paper triangle and sealed it with crumbs of black bread. When the train stopped at one of the stations, Rakhil stood up on the plank and through the barred window saw two signal women standing on the tracks. She waved to them and threw the letter. One of the women immediately turned away, but the other one followed the flying piece of paper with her eyes and nodded to Rakhil.

When Rakhil described this moment to me, it seemed like a slow motion scene: a flying piece of paper and the long gaze of a woman following it. What a scene for a movie!

And the kind soul did not nod in vain. The letter arrived! Sulamith decided that God spoke to her to help her save her sister. She put on her best suit and attached to it the "Honorary Award" she had just received (a rarity at that time). She made her way to the reception of the Cheka office and begged for the permission to visit her sister and at least bring her child home. Then, permission in hand, she undertook an arduous journey of thousands of miles to the "Algeria" camp.

On learning of her sister's visit Rakhil was stuck dumb. When she recovered, she realized that Sulamith wanted to take Azari away. Although she wanted him free, she also knew that this could lead to her own premature death at the camps. As a nursing mother she was able to avoid hard labour duties at the camp. As they had to communicate in front of the camp's commandant, the sisters understood each other's predicament without words. At the end of the meeting Mita said that the boy was still too weak to withstand a long journey home and asked for permission to send food parcels to them. Mita was granted permission to send parcels, and she headed back to Moscow, to try to further alleviate the fate of her sister.

Could she somehow reduce the sentence or rescue Rakhil and Azari from the Gulag altogether? Alas, there was little hope. In Moscow there was a rumor that at one reception in the Kremlin after the concert, Stalin proposed a toast to Rakhil's brother Asaf Messerer.

Was this true? Many years later in New York I asked Asaf about this incident and he confirmed it. He and ballerina Olga Lepeshinskaya were regarded as the leading pair at the Bolshoi and were occasionally invited to participate in concerts in the Kremlin. One day after such a concert, Asaf and a group of artists were sitting at a banquet table talking, when he suddenly felt ill at ease: it seemed that everyone was staring at him. He turned back and saw Stalin standing behind him. Asaf was about to get up when Stalin patted him on the shoulder and said: "Great dancing. Very high jump! Here you are," and he pointed to Lepeshinskaya, "she is like a dragonfly, and you—you are like an "orlik" [an eagle]". At that moment Voroshilov interrupted Stalin and he was momentarily distracted, but soon after he came back to Asaf, raised his glass and said that he drinks to his health. Asaf was stunned by this manifestation of the "royal favor" and was not sure how to respond. But Stalin already moved away.

The family asked Asaf to help Rakhil since he received such high praise from Stalin. Shortly thereafter Asaf was invited to organize a festive concert in the club of the NKVD. Ironically, this club is located on the same street as the infamous Lubyanka prison. At that time it played a considerable role in the cultural life of Moscow. The Club belonged to a most powerful (and wealthy) organization, had a huge hall for performances, and only the absolutely best of the artistic elite were invited to perform. Once you were invited, it was unthinkable to refuse.

In early 1939 Asaf was sitting at the NKVD Club at the premiere of a performance that he had directed. He began talking to his neighbour and learned that this person was working under no other than the Deputy Secretary of NKVD. Asaf, who had so convincingly played heroic roles on the stage, was in reality very shy. One can imagine how hard it would have been for him to take such a bold step as to ask the man to talk to his chief and arrange a meeting to discuss a personal matter. He suggested that it would be better if his sister went to the meeting as she would be more familiar with the case. Perhaps the success of his production and the fact that Asaf was greeted with a standing ovation when he came onto the stage had an effect as the neighbor did arrange an audience for Mita with the Deputy Secretary (who was later also shot as the purges began to take their toll on the perpetrators as well).

Sulamith eloquently described him all the tribulations of Rakhil and her baby and achieved the unimaginable: Rakhil's camp sentence was replaced by an exile in Kazakhstan, namely in the town of Chimkent. Moreover, Mita was allowed to go to the camp and personally help to relocate her sister to her place of exile!

Chimkent was the farthest Central Asian town in the region, where, during long summer days people suffered from scorching heat exacerbated by myriads of flies. In addition to the local Kazakh population, there were many exiles, among them people like Rakhil, widowed women with children. There was a cultural club where Rakhil immediately set up and organized a ballet troupe. Although she had not had professional ballet education, she attended numerous performances and rehearsals at the Bolshoi and the Ballet School and knew popular dances, such as the Dance of Little Swans. Later, Maya Plisetskaya participated in one performance when she visited her mother during holidays.

Beautiful and still young, Rakhil attracted many local men who wanted to marry her, but she believed that her beloved husband would return one day and did not reciprocate their intentions. Once she received a parcel with Chocolates, "Mishka in the North", which she apparently had not tasted before. The originator of this brand, also of the chocolates, "Squirrel" brand, was a famous theater director , Natalia Sats, whose husband, before he was arrested and shot, was the Minister for food production in the country. She once jokingly told me during an interview that people would remember her because of these chocolates. So, Rakhil decided that Mita had sent those candies as a sign that her Mikhail (Mishka is short for Mikhail) had returned to Spitsbergen, and she might soon see him. Like many other women, she did not understand the meaning of the monstrous Stalin's sentence , "Ten years incommunicado," which actually meant death by a firing squad. By this time Mikhail Plisetsky had already been shot. Only four decades later, Rakhil received the documentary evidence of her husband's death and the subsequent rehabilitation:

"Dear Rakhil Mikhaylovna!"—a certain A. Nikonov, head of the secretariat of the Military Collegium of the Supreme Court of the USSR, wrote in 1989, "Enclosed is the information you requested: Mikhail Emmanuilovich Plisetsky, born in 1899, member of the CPSU (Bolshevik) from 1919, until his arrest, manager of the Trust "Arctic Coal" was unjustly sentenced to death on Jan. 8, 1938, on false charges of espionage and sabotage by involvement in the anti-Soviet terrorist organization. The sentence was carried out. This happened immediately after the verdict, on January 8, 1938... Further investigation carried out in 1955-56, showed that M. E. Plisetsky was wrongly convicted..." The execution by firing squad was sanctioned by Zhdanov, Molotov, Kaganovich and Voroshilov. Their names appear on the title page of the so-called "Stalin's hit list". We know now the place of the execution and the burial site, the notorious NKVD "Kommunarka", near Moscow.

Mikhail died in the prime of his life, without any idea that his daughter Maya Plisetskaya would be destined to become a world-famous ballerina. Rakhil forever remained single and hated the bloody Stalinist regime, which deprived her and her children of a father, a regime that destroyed millions of lives... She taught this hatred for the injustice to mankind, and also she inculcated the will to Maya and to her sons, and to us, her relatives, to stand up to Stalin and his henchmen.

Rakhil returned to Moscow two months before the start of the World War II and moved with Sulamith and her husband to where Maya lived, a tiny two-room communal apartment in Schepkinsky Proezd, behind the Bolshoi Theater. Rakhil and Azari slept on a camp bed that was unfolded at night-time near the door. However, such conditions seemed to her a veritable paradise after the camp conditions and the miserable hovels in Chimkent where she spent years.

She was also happy to see her daughter's triumph at a ballet school concert. Maya Plisetskaya believes that this "Impromptu" performance staged by Leonid Yakobson was of a particular importance in her career as she "transformed from a novice ballet student into an independent, mature , and daring professional ballerina." A few months after the start of the war, Rakhil and the children evacuated to Sverdlovsk, in the Urals, where she managed, with great difficulty, to get a job of a registrar at a local health clinic that enabled her to receive coupons to buy food for the children. Rakhil gave me a packet of letters she received from her relatives who were scattered throughout the country during the war. Unfortunately, letters from Rakhil are missing, but letters from her loved ones survive and demonstrate that she was the major link between all family members; her boundless wisdom and compassion helped them to endure hardships. I was especially moved by the letters from her father, Mikhail Borisovich, to his son, my father, Emmanuel Messerer, who died during a German bombing raid when he was on duty patrolling the roof of a Moscow home. This tragedy was concealed from my grandfather. The letters were returned to him with a stamp of "unknown addressee" and he begged Rakhil to explain the silence from Nulia, as they called my father. Rakhil tried to pacify him and distract him in her letters, blaming the inefficiency of postal services in wartime.

In a letter from Elizabeth on February 16, 1942, it is apparent that Rakhil tried to send a parcel to her older brother, Mattaniy, a Professor, who languished in Gulag. Rakhilinka, my sunshine. I've shed many tears when reading your letter. How awful to learn about our great misfortune, the loss of our beloved Nulia. I won't ask you for details, not to aggravate the matter....Also I am deeply disturbed to read about the plight of Mattaniy. What can we do? Two days ago I received a postcard from him. He asked me to send him a parcel. He asks for some sugar, rusks and tobacco. It is very painful. I feel real pain when I think of him. I can send him a food parcel, except for the sugar. But they allow parcels to be sent only to the front and not within the country. Perhaps you will have better luck in sending it? I will still try... Do keep in touch; it is such joy to receive letters from you."

And here is an excerpt from Asaf's letter who was evacuated into Kuibyshev where he managed the Bolshoi Theatre troupe: "Dear Rakhilinka. I received your letter asking about accommodation in Kuibyshev. The housing issue is very tough here. It is almost impossible to find a room, and the only way is to move into the hostel of the

Bolshoi Theater. I think I will be able to organize this, but, please, keep in mind that there are 20-25 people living in one room... Also I am very concerned about the epidemic of typhus. Firstly, you can get infected on the train, and secondly, it might be difficult to gain the entry to Kuibyshev."

Rakhil wanted to move to Kuibyshev because of Maya who missed on her ballet lessons for one year and it was important for her to continue her studies. But soon Rakhil learnt that part of the troupe had returned to Moscow and, according to rumors, the ballet school classes resumed. She took a great risk to let her sixteen-year old daughter go to Moscow, despite the dangers and perils of coming to the capital without a special pass. She wanted Maya to join Sulamith who had been invited to participate in the first Moscow ballet performances during the war. Fortunately, Maya was able to enter the graduation class and soon she began to perform in The Bolshoi as the theatre was in need of soloists at that time.

I remember Rakhil immediately after the war. Her sons, who studied at the Bolshoi Ballet School, spent summers at a summer camp, in Polenovo, near famous Tarusa. Rakhil got a job there. I was also taken to this camp though I was only 6 years old. It was the first time for me to be away from home for three months and, thanks to Rakhil, this experience was not so traumatic. She treated me like a mother as I sought her comfort after every boyish conflict.

Since then, all my life, I loved her as a second mother. When our communal apartment was renovated, I asked to live with Rakhil in their communal apartment at Schepkinsky Proezd. The family accepted me despite the congestion, and I slept on the bed between two famous ballerinas—Maya and Sulamith. Mom's brother, who lived with us, joked that from an early age, I showed a great promise with women. I did not understand of course what he meant.

In the 60's, Sulamith started taking long trips abroad, mostly to Japan, where she founded the first classical ballet school, naming it after Tchaikovsky. She left her son Mikhail with Rakhil, knowing that her sister would take good care of him and look after his education. There was never a limit to Rakhil's motherly love for everyone. (Recently

Mikhail Messerer has been appointed the chief choreographer of the Mikhailovsky Theater in St. Petersburg and continues to work as a teacher at the Royal Ballet in London).

A film director, Basil Katanyan, Maya Plisetskaya's friend, who often visited her in her house wrote in his book Touching the Idols: "I am very fond of her mother, Rakhil Mikhailovna, such a decent, good woman. I admire her gift to do many things at once: cooking, cleaning, etc., with every family member having a different schedule. Maya goes to ballet classes and her garments have to be ironed. Alex comes home from rehearsals, the junior needs help with his homework ... She is always responsive and expeditious."

Boris Pevzner, the nephew of Rakhil's husband recalls:

"My mother, Mikhail's first cousin, was a good friend of Rakhil; and after Misha's arrest, their relations became even closer. During the war, at the end of 1943, we moved to Moscow and often visited Rara, as my mother called her, at the house behind the Bolshoi. I remember that in one room, where Maya lived, there hung on a long hoop a rather modernistic lampshade made by her, and in the other room, toy railway cars, made by seven year old Azari, ran on the floor. After we moved to Leningrad, I would visit Rakhil whenever I came to Moscow, even after the death of my mother in 1964. She always met me with great hospitality, and I felt her kindred warmth. If I was lucky, and Maya was dancing on that day, Rakhil would take me with her to see the ballet. Because of her, I saw the four famous ballets of Shchedrin— Plisetskaya: Carmen suite, Anna Karenina, Seagul, and The Lady with a Lap Dog . She took a keen interest in my family, and in my life. I felt that it was a true interest, that the more she learned about her relatives, the fuller her life became. She will always stay in my memory as a very energetic and kind person, with a warm smile.

Rakhil was fully involved in all aspects of her children's life: the triumphs on the stage as well as their turbulent times. Rakhil deeply felt for Maya's troubles in the 50's, for example. Maya wrote that at the time she was on the verge of a suicide: for six years, the KGB suspected her of spying because of her one brief meeting with a British diplomat. She was not allowed to travel abroad. British, American, and French impresarios demanded Maya to be included in the Bolshoi Ballet tours, but the Goskoncert always announced at the last minute that, for one reason or another, she allegedly could not go. Thanks to her mother's moral support, Maya survived this terrible period. She also writes that together with her husband, a prominent composer, Rodion Shchedrin, they managed to secure a small apartment in 1958 largely due to the efforts of her mother whose "personality, although gentle, showed determination in the extreme." And it is true that for the sake of her children, Rakhil was ready to fight any bureaucratic obstacles till the end.

In the 70's, there was a fierce struggle between two camps at the Bolshoi Theater, the one of Maya Plisetskaya, and the other of Yuri Grigorovich, the artistic director of the Bolshoi Ballet, an authoritarian figure who managed the Bolshoi ballet and who would not allow leading choreographers to take part in the production of ballet performances. This animosity had an impact on the ballet careers of both Maya's brothers: Azari and Alexander. Grigorovich, in every way he could, hampered their progress in the theater, and they were forced to leave Moscow for a long period. Rakhil suffered a great deal from this separation from them. And, of course, the worst tragedy in her life was the early death of her son, Alexander Plisetsky, who suffered from heart disease. He did not survive to take up the invitation from a well-known surgeon in America who promised to perform surgery on him. He died during surgery at a Moscow hospital. Rakhil's health rapidly deteriorated after this tragedy.

Rakhil's life was full of great sadnesses as well as great joys. She never missed a single performance in which her children, Maya, Alexander and Azari, participated. Rakhil would sit in the front row, alongside her younger brother, Alexander, next to the famous Lily Brik (the muse of the poet Mayakovsky) wearing one of her beautiful black dresses, smiling at the many admirers of her children who came to pay their respects during intermissions. Sometimes she would give them family photographs, signing "A memento from Maya's mother."

Towards the end of her life, Rakhil got the opportunity to travel. She stayed in England with her sister, Sulamith, who was awarded an OBE for her contribution to British culture. She spent six months in Cuba, where Azari worked, as well as time in France and Spain. In her ninetieth year she came to America, accompanied by her brother Alexander, who tenderly looked after her, and actually helped extend her life.

In the US they lived in a beautiful house that belonged to Mr. Stanley Plesent, Rakhil's husband's nephew. The house was located on the beach at Larchmont, one of the most beautiful suburbs of New York. In the mornings and the evenings, she always looked beautiful and majestic even in her old age, sitting in the front garden, with neighbors passing by and stopping to exchange a few words with her. They called her "The Queen of Larchmont". The two Plesent brothers, Stanley and Manny, carefully preserved the relics of their father Lester's visit to Moscow in 1934: a book about the labor feat on Spitsbergen with a patriotic inscription by Mikhail Plisetsky, and a ritual tallis that was given to Lester before he left Moscow. And of course, they cherish the photos of Rakhil made during her visit to America.

Rakhil died at the age of 91 and was buried in the family grave at Novodevichy Cemetery in Moscow, at the start of the famous Cherry Orchard avenue. Her brother, the acclaimed MKhAT (Moscow Art Theater) actor Azary, was the first to be buried there in 1937. Rakhil named her youngest son, who was born the same year, after him. This family tomb is located next to the graves of Chekhov, Levitan, Stanislavsky, and Gogol. And nowadays, just like at the nearby graves of these cultural icons of Russia, there are flowers placed on her grave by some unknown person. It seems that to this day Muscovites still remember Rakhil.

GIFTS EXCHANGED WITH PAUL SCOFIELD

Azary Messerer

The lights are dimming, the curtain is about to rise, and few among the audience are paying any attention to the public announcement reminding them that audio and video taping of the performance is strictly forbidden. Yet for me this announcement evokes a vivid memory of my favorite actor, Paul Scofield. I recall how he called "priceless" the gift that I gave him in Moscow. Did he know that he also gave me a priceless gift, not just of his time and his talent, but of his integrity, which possibly saved my career and maybe even my freedom?

Paul Scofield was the first eminent English actor to come on tour to the USSR. It was 1956, and I was 16. I was preparing to enter the Institute of Foreign Languages, was studying English enthusiastically, and for me the arrival of Shakespeare troupe, led by Peter Brooke, a young but already world-famous director, bringing his production of Hamlet, was a great event. I wasn't able to get a ticket, but intended to buy one from a 'scalper'. I heard that the performance would be in an "affiliated hall" of the theater, and so I arrived in advance at another address of the Bolshoi on Pushkin Street, which I frequented. No excessive crowding there; you could even buy tickets at the box office.

But going up to the window, I discovered that that night's performance was not Hamlet, but an operetta, Sylvia. It turned out that Hamlet was playing at an affiliated hall of MKhAT (Moscow Art Theater) on Moskvin Street, about 15 minute walk away. I took off at great speed, but alas, MKhAT was a different story altogether: hordes of people were looking to buy an extra ticket, and only ten minutes left until the curtain rose. I didn't get a ticket to the performance and was despondent.

The next day I found out that my famous cousin, prima ballerina Maya Plisetskaya, had a ticket. Luckily, she was performing that night and, after I described to her vividly what happened the day before, she gave me the ticket. I decided that fate was smiling on me; I experienced such unexpected manifestations of grace several times in connection with Paul Scofield.

All day before the performance I studied Hamlet in English, and read the soliloquies over and over again. But when I witnessed his acting for the first time, he astounded me by the fact that in his mouth, or so it seemed, familiar words sounded uncommon ; he put accents where I didn't anticipate them; he spoke certain lines very quickly; occasionally his voice would almost die away on words which scaled into long pauses. What's more, it seemed to me, he didn't speak, but sang. One could listen to his voice, divorced from the text, as if to music. It was mesmerizing. Maybe all English actors play Shakespeare this way, I thought. But no, his fellow actors were not capable of this.

Scofield possessed a unique voice in terms of its power, range and beauty of timbre and no metaphor can actually do it justice. The director, Fred Zinnemann, tried: "When he begins talking, it puts me in mind of a Rolls Royce being started." The critic, J.C. Trewin, likened Scofield's voice to "sunlight on a broken column." Scofield's face was strikingly expressive, with a Roman profile. At times it became frozen, at times aroused, like a dormant volcano erupting, the actor exploding in fury. Striking too were his majestic form (6 feet 2 inches tall), and his laugh, now tender, now diabolic, full of mockery and hate.

I had never before seen such great acting, and I left the performance as if in a trance. It was art at its best. His amazing performance was a breakthrough in the country's cultural history during the Cold War isolation. Two years later they were writing about another breakthrough in connection with Van Cliburn's triumph at the Tchaikovsky Piano Competition. But Scofield was the first Western artist who satisfied the hunger that the Moscow public felt for foreign art. He returned home a hero and was soon honoured as a Commander of the British Empire.

Having entered the Institute of Foreign Languages, I began to work with Radio Moscow, broadcasting to England. I wrote and voiced programs directed at young people. In the radio's sound archives, I unexpectedly found a recording of that play, copied Scofield's Hamlet's soliloquies, and listened to them, entranced. I memorized them, and when the Institute announced a competition for the best reading of verse and prose in English, I volunteered. For two years in a row I won the First prize, reading the two Hamlet soliloquies. It's unlikely the admission committee knew I was copying Scofield. I read with such feeling that the narration became mine. I knew that no one could truly imitate Scofield's voice.

With these successes, it seemed that fate smiled on me again and I fancied myself an actor. I found out that the popular Moscow University Theater had announced an audition and I began to prepare for it. They required a prose selection and I chose Garshin's tale, The Traveling Frog, which turned out somewhat prophetic for me since it was, after all, about emigration that I was to experience later. As for the required soliloquy, I had to, of course, read my favorite one from Hamlet: "What's Hecuba to him, or he to Hecuba. . .?" which the Danish prince delivers after the performance of the traveling player who so impressed him.

I tried to read it in Russian, with the same intonations as Scofield, but nothing came of it. It sounded artificial. In my memory I heard the soliloquy only in English. I had given up completely when a friend came up with an idea, "Why don't you read in English? They've heard it so many times at competitions they're probably sick of it, but this will be something original." At the audition I recited Garshin's tale quite well, and then modestly requested the opportunity to read the soliloquy in English. The committee conferred and then gave me permission. I was in great shape and rendered the unhappy Hecuba with special flair, with dramatic pauses. The committee was quite impressed. I was accepted unanimously. What's more, Vsevolod Shestakov, one of the leading actors of the theater, the husband of Iya Savina, at that time the star of the University Theater, offered me the main part in Leonid Zorin's play Clear May, which he intended to stage.

I was to play the role of a young, talented writer, and the action began with my having to endlessly and passionately kiss my leading lady, played by a beautiful graduating student of the Economics Department, Alla Demidova . Alas, at that time I was a shy lad and unable to kiss passionately. And besides, Alla, the future top star of the Russian theater , was rather indifferent towards me. Between us, as they say, there was no chemistry. I was also discouraged by my friend Anatoly Makarov, who, after the next rehearsal said offhandedly, "You're playing perhaps a future Russian Hemingway... you get it? But what kind of Hemingway are you?" Indeed, I didn't measure up to a young Soviet Hemingway. Incidentally, Anatoly Makarov himself later became a writer and a famous journalist for Izvestia's supplement The Week.

We worked for a long time and finally got to the final rehearsal, where the famous playwright himself showed up. He criticized the staging mercilessly, and the premiere didn't take place. And with this, my brief acting career was over. I realized I'd never become a Scofield. To do so, one had to give the whole of one's soul to the theater, all one's thoughts and time and, naturally, one had to have a great talent. I didn't want to be a second-rate actor.

It was during the Shakespeare Theater's second visit in 1964, when they presented King Lear, directed by that very same Peter Brook , that I came to understand what separated a mediocre, or even a good actor, from Scofield. By then I had been working for two years broadcasting to England and was preparing carefully for the Theater's arrival. With difficulty, I managed to persuade the authorities to give me an assignment to cover the tour, write reports, and conduct behind-the-scenes interviews. Having received permission for the trip, I traveled to Leningrad where the tour began. They had booked a room for me at the Astoria hotel, opposite St. Isaac's Cathedral, where the English were staying. Even before the beginning of the tour I was able to interview no fewer than ten actors. They all spoke with a sigh whenever the conversation turned to Scofield, pointing upward, as if he hovered above them at some unreachable height, where truly great art resides. In the Hermitage I conversed with the brilliant Peter Brook, a man of irrepressible energy. He showed me a long list he had prepared in England of things he intended to accomplish on breaks between rehearsals and performances: seeing a Russian wedding in a church, viewing Levitan's and Repin's paintings, attending rehearsals in the theaters, including the theater of Satire, whose lead director, Pluchek, was his cousin (Brook's father, a scholar, emigrated from Russia before the Revolution), meeting with actors playing Chekhov—he intended to stage The Cherry Orchard—and much more. Naturally, I asked him about his collaboration with Scofield, to which he responded paradoxically, "Paul would listen to you, let you explain with all your creative fervour something you think is absolutely right, then do the exact opposite and make you realize that this is what you meant. That's creative collaboration." Brook also recounted how Scofield worked painstakingly, even agonizingly, over every role. He struggled with Hamlet for a long time. This is how Brook described Scofield when he finally found his character. "The door opened and a small man entered. He was wearing a black suit, steel-rimmed glasses, and holding a suitcase. We wondered why this stranger was wandering on our stage. Then we realized it was Paul, transformed. His tall body had shrunk, his hair cut short, he had become insignificant." Brook added that the role of King Lear was Scofield's greatest achievement.

It's hard to imagine his acting better than in that Hamlet of 1956. But in King Lear I saw a figure so distant from Hamlet that at first I couldn't believe it was Scofield. I knew him only by his voice, so strong that it drowned all the other voices, but this time Scofield's voice seemed sharp and unpleasant. One could even appreciate the two daughters' malice toward the king, who was unhinged, demanding unquestioning submission, in a word, a tyrant. In the second act Scofield's Lear begins to change and, transformed by ingratitude and cruelty he himself experiences, becomes human, now deserving of sympathy and compassion. In the last scene of madness, Scofield showed the tragedy of a powerful man, crushed by his folly. Forty years later the actors of the Shakespeare Theater dispensed justice in the so-called Hamburg calculation: by secret ballot they had to decide who played Shakespeare best of all. They gave Scofield the top prize for the role of King Lear, even though the great masters of English theater, Laurence Olivier and John Gielgud, were competing with him (both of whom, incidentally, I also had the good fortune to interview in Moscow). Explaining their decision, a theater representative said, "Compared to Scofield, Laurence

Olivier was lacking in depth and soul, John Gielgud was deficient in physical energy and sense of danger." Scofield agreed to grant me an interview the very next day after the premiere, so that I was able, before the start of the Moscow tour, to submit the material for the radio and for a long article to the newspaper Sovetskaya Kultura. I also was able to send to the newspaper by fast train, (the so-called The Red Arrow, running between Leningrad and Moscow) two photos which Scofield gave me as a present. On one photo he is as he was then— handsome, with thick chestnut hair as yet untouched by gray, and calm, knowing gaze. He had recently turned 40. On the other photo, a furrowed face, in his eyes the sorrow and despair of a Lear. Both these photos illustrated the article published on April 2, 1964.

At the start of the interview I reminded him of the critic Kenneth Tynan's remark that Scofield had the ability to widen the scope of his role until it met his standards. Scofield replied, "I never ponder over whether a given role is right for me and whether I am right for a given role. For me the most important thing is to understand the character and make it so clear to the audience that the spectator suddenly feels: "I actually know this man." The audience must forget it is separated from the Shakespearean hero by four centuries. Directors and actors are obliged to transmit Shakespeare's thoughts and emotions in such a way as if they were the thoughts and emotions of our contemporaries."

"Like every English actor, I was brought up on Shakespeare from childhood, knew King Lear by heart in grade school, saw many splendid actors playing the title role. That made it more difficult for me to forget everything I knew about Lear and read the Shakespearean tragedy anew, as if for the first time. This was essential, or else I could not make King Lear live."

"Which was the first Shakespearean role you played on the stage?"

"Juliet. Yes, don't be surprised. I was thirteen at the time. In certain English schools they kept the tradition of Shakespearean times—boys playing both male and female parts. I was very embarrassed when they dressed me in a woman's wig with long, fair hair. But this first role decided my fate. I realized that more than anything I wanted to become an actor," he said.

When I asked whether he intended to play Hamlet again, Scofield replied that he was already too old for the part. You have to play Hamlet before you're 40. At the same time, he regretted that nothing remained of Brook's superb production. That it hadn't been filmed. Then I mentioned to him that there was, thank god, at least a fine audio tape, which I listened to often. Scofield was very surprised, and I realized that Hamlet was recorded in Moscow without the permission of the cast. One can even assume that since it was the first tour of a Western troupe, those who did the recording didn't know they were breaking the rules. It was obvious he read my thoughts instantly and, smiling, remarked that such a tape would be a priceless gift for him. I asked for his autograph and he took out the two of his famous photos that I mentioned before, and signed them both. (To this day one of them hangs on the wall in my house.)

En route back to Moscow I became uneasy. How can I hand over the cassette to Scofield, would he tell about this recording to the press, and would this cause a scandal that would ruin my career and maybe my life? But I didn't doubt Scofield's integrity. I had to trust that he understood everything and would not want to ruin me. As for informing the press, I already had read a good deal about his shyness, his reluctance to give interviews, his indifference to fame and sensation. Not without reason, in almost every article about him, they called him a "private person." Once he answered a journalist on the phone, "This is Scofield, a private person." Unfortunately, the word 'privacy' has no adequate translation into Russian. How can one, for example, translate the common expression: "It violates my privacy?" It violates my right to a private life. No, it simply doesn't translate well. Is it because the whole concept is so alien to the Russian psyche, bred under the collectivist mentality for so long? Scofield refused the title of 'Sir' bestowed on him by his knighthood because he rejected the caste system in the English theater. As he said, why should other actors be called simply "Mister" but the select few, such as him, Gielgud or Olivier, "Sir"? "If you want to have a title, what's wrong with "Mr."? If you have always been that, then why lose your title? I have the title which is the same I've ever had. But it's not political. I have a CBE, which I accept very gratefully."

115

I'll never forget Scofield's radiant smile when I gave him the tape in a bouquet of flowers. I found out four years later that he was pleased with the tape. As before, I came to interview him for the radio and Sovetskaya Kultura newspaper. This time there was no "privacy". I was joined by a photographer and the editor of the theater section (I had to co-author the article with her, and it was published December 16, 1967). On the photo featured in the paper, Scofield was captured with a pipe in hand, gazing thoughtfully at a cloud of smoke. He had grown a tuft of beard, his face had wrinkled, and his temples were graying. There were noticeable bags under his eyes. "I am tired," he said. "Before leaving for Moscow, Laurence Olivier advised me not to play Macbeth twice in one day, but I didn't listen to him and played him three times in forty-eight hours. I couldn't refuse the Moscow public, which I love very much."

It's possible that Macbeth is a most difficult role, indeed. I found out that British actors have a superstitious fear of it. For example, one doesn't utter lines from Macbeth backstage. They say it brings misfortune.

"Oh yes, in Macbeth there's something incomprehensible. He is indeed truly terrifying. To play him honestly, you must not evoke sympathy for him. By no means, unless it is pity. Of the kind, 'You poor thing, you made a mistake and I feel sorry for you. I wouldn't want to be in your shoes.' No one would dream of putting himself in his place. It's impossible to conceive. It's also true that in the second half of the play, the figure somehow loses intensity, because Macbeth loses his heart. And so the main difficulty is for the audience to see, feel and understand how a man loses his heart."

Scofield came to Moscow in 1967 for the last time at the height of his fame not only in the theater, but also in film. Few before were honoured with the highest award in both genres. Scofield got one, a Tony, in 1965, for playing Sir Thomas Moore in Robert Bolt's play A Man for all Seasons. A year later, when Zinnemanns's film came out, based on the play, he received an Oscar for best actor. Scofield's nobility was embodied in the figure of Moore, in whom, I think, he was really playing himself. Moore goes to his execution knowing that by refusing to bend to the will of the usurper-King Henry VIII, he has carried out his duty. He goes to his execution with an inner clarity, preserving to the end his dignity and honour.

"Thomas More," said Scofield, "is one of my most beloved heroes. I admire his integrity, his strength of conviction, the beauty of his ethics. Moore's thinking had an enormous influence on the history of England. Actually, I succeeded in this role because, side by side with Shakespearian roles, I acted in a lot of contemporary plays."

In fact, Scofield created a whole gallery of contemporary and non-Shakespearian characters, both in the theater and in film, tragic, as well as highly comic. As regards to the latter, his favorite role was Gogol's Khlestakov. "I took great pleasure in playing Khlestakov, an incredibly funny braggart. His dissembling is simply splendid. This is genuine comedy and I really love playing in comedies."

In addition to Khlestakov, Scofield played in many other Russian roles. There was Chekhov's Treplev in The Seagull, Vershinin in The Three Sisters, and Uncle Vanya. Also, Karenin in the televised film Anna Karenina, Alexander Shcherbatov in the film 1919, Sergei Diaghilev in the film Nijinsky—an unfinished project, and a Russian officer in the film Scorpio, where he starred with the great American actor Burt Lancaster. Such a diversity of roles, and also the mastery of a character actor, allowed Scofield to perform until ripe old age. True, he often no longer played leading roles, but rather supporting ones. For example, in the movie version of Hamlet by the Italian director Franco Zeffirelli, he appeared as an apparition, the ghost of Hamlet's father, but acted so powerfully, that Hamlet, Mel Gibson, against this background, seemed almost inconsequential. Gibson himself said, "When I played with Scofield, I felt I was being thrown into the ring with Mike Tyson". (This was in 1990, when Tyson was a world champion.) Scofield told me about his life outside the theater. He said proudly that Martin, his son, was more educated than he and knew Shakespeare better. At that time Martin had just graduated from Oxford, and went on to become a professor of philology. His daughter, Sara, road horseback better than he, he said, and they often set off riding on horseback around rural England. Scofield lived his whole life in Sussex and did not want to exchange his own domain for Hollywood, although this was offered to him time and again. He evidently was afraid of damaging his stable personal life—he had lived more than sixty years with the actress Joan Parker. Unfortunately, as a consequence, he often had to refuse excellent roles in the movies. In the theater he played the part of Salieri in Amadeus brilliantly, and of course was the first choice for this role in the film. But in the end, the role went to Murray Abraham, made him famous, and garnered an Oscar for him.

Paul Scofield died in 2008, at the age of 86. Great number of obituaries and remembrances appeared in the world press, which, by analogy with the film, were collected on the Internet under the heading "An Actor for all Seasons." Richard Eyre, the director of the National Theater, was the most succinct, "He is not simply the best, but the best of all, who ever acted." Others wrote of the influence the great actor had on them. I can add my modest voice to theirs because Paul Scofield for me was a personal ideal of an actor and a great human being.

The Art of
Translation

Exegi monumentum:
Poems by Russian Writers on a
Horatian Theme

Peter France

Not long ago, knowing I was translating poems by Konstantin
Batyushkov, my friend Ilya Kutik drew my attention to one of the few
poems written during the years of his mental illness. This extraordinary
piece, entitled "Imitation of Horace", was included in a letter to a
friend, and only published long after the poet's death. I couldn't
resist the temptation of putting it into English, and when I had done
this, placing it alongside two of the most famous Russian "versions"
of the same theme, those of Derzhavin and Pushkin, which I had
previously translated. Thanks to Boris Dralyuk, they are published
together here, preceded by Horace's Latin (Odes III. 30), the literal
English translation by C. E. Bennett (from Horace, *Odes and Epodes*,
Loeb Classical Library, 1946) and one further translation, my version
of Lomonosov's translation of Horace, which set the whole Russian
sequence in motion. Ilya Kutik then offers a detailed examination of
the development of this topos in Russian poetry. Kutik's essay refers
to the Russian texts; I have tried to keep close to the Russian (slightly
closer than in earlier versions published elsewhere), but my translations
are meant to be read as poems rather than as cribs. So where details of
the Russian are changed or omitted in the English, I have pointed this
out in parenthetical notes in bold.

121

HORACE (c. 23 BC)

Exegi monumentum aere perennius
regalique situ pyramidum altius,
quod non imber edax, non Aquilo impotens
possit diruere aut innumerabilis
annorum series et fuga temporum.
non omnis moriar multaque pars mei
vitabit Libitinam : usque ego postera
crescam laude recens. dum Capitolium
scandet cum tacita virgine pontifex,
dicar, qua violens obstrepit Aufidus
et qua pauper aquae Daunus agrestium
regnavit populorum, ex humile potens
princeps Aeolium carmen ad Italos
deduxisse modos. sume superbiam
quaesitam meritis, et mihi Delphica
lauro cinge volens, Melpomene, comam.

[I have finished a monument more lasting than bronze and loftier than the Pyramids' royal pile, one that no wasting rain, no furious north wind can destroy, or the countless chain of years and the ages' flight. I shall not altogether die, but a mighty part of me shall escape the death-goddess. On and on I shall grow, ever fresh with the glory of after time. So long as the Pontiff climbs the Capitol with the silent Vestal, I, risen high from low estate, where wild Aufidus thunders and where Daunus in a parched land once ruled o'er a peasant folk, shall be famed for having been the first to adapt Aeolian song to Italian verse. Accept the proud honour won by thy merits, Melpomene, and graciously crown my locks with Delphic bays.]

MIKHAILO LOMONOSOV (1747)

I have built myself a mark of immortality
Loftier than pyramids, stronger than copper,
One that fierce Boreas will never destroy,
Nor multitudes of ages, nor the sharp teeth of time.
I shall not wholly die, but death will leave behind
A mighty part of me, when life is gone.
Everywhere I shall increase in honour
While mighty Rome still possesses the world.
Where the swift waters of Aufidus roar,
Where Daurus once ruled a simple people,
My fatherland will not be dumb to say
That my humble parentage did not bar me
From bringing to Italy Aeolian verse
And making music with the lyre of Alcaeus.
Be proud, Muse, of your true deserving
And crown my head with Delphic laurel.

*

GAVRILA DERZHAVIN (1795)

I have built myself a monument miraculous, eternal,
Stronger than metal, higher than pyramids;
Whirlwind and thunder will not overthrow it;
It will not be destroyed by flying years.

So! I shall not all die; my greater part,
Fleeing corruption, will survive my death,
My fame will grow and spread and never fade
While still the Slavs are honoured here on earth.

My name will run from the White to the Black Sea,
Where Volga, Don, Neva and Ural flow;
Those peoples' songs will guard my memory,
How from an unknown birth I became known

For being the first to dare in sprightly verse
To tell all Russia of Felitsa's worth,
The first to talk of God in simple words
And with a smile to speak the truth to tsars.

Oh muse! Be rightly proud of your exploits.
If any scorn you, scorn them in your turn,
And with a free unhurried hand exalt
This brow with immortality's new dawn.

*

ALEKSANDR PUSHKIN (1836)

I have built myself a monument not made
By hands, the people will surround it,
Imperishably holding up its head
    Higher than Alexander's column.

I shall not wholly die: my soul will live
In sacred tunes, beyond the grave's oblivion;
I shall be known as long as in this world
    There is a single poet living.

I shall be spoken of in Russian lands;
My name will find a place in every language
Spoken by the proud Slavs, the Finns, the sons
    Of the wild Tunguz and the Kalmyks.

And by the people I shall long be loved,
For with my lyre I stirred their tender feelings,
Proclaiming freedom in a cruel age
    And charity for the defeated.

Muse, be obedient to the will of God:
Not fearing insults, not demanding honour,
Accept both praise and slander with a nod
    And with the fool don't deign to quarrel.

*

KONSTANTIN BATYUSHKOV (1826?)

I have built a huge, miraculous monument,
Singing your praises: it will not see death!
Like your sweet image, charming, benevolent
(Witness Napoleon, our faithful friend)
I shan't see death. All I have done in letters,
Dodging oblivion will live in print.
Not Phoebus, I alone have forged these fetters
Where I can keep the universe shut in.
I was the first who dared to speak in Russian
Amusingly about Elise's virtue,
To chat with true simplicity of God
And thunder truth to tsars for their own good.
Be stars for us, my empress, my tsaritsas!
Tsars are not stars: Mount Pindus is *my* state,
Venus my sister, you my little sister,
    My Caesar—scissors in the hands of Fate.

RUSSIAN "MONUMENTS": THESES AND REFLECTIONS

Ilya Kutik

I.

Up to the present day, those who are *outside* Russian poetry, want (or expect) it to provide *great meanings* to nourish the people—and also individual heroism, of course, and the early (or violent, i.e. *tragic*) death of its dramatis personae. *Anachronism* (or *archaism* of thought) is a massive phenomenon, but this is not what we are talking about here. But why keep waiting for Godot, when these great meanings have already found their conscious place in Russian poetry? If you look at it *from within*, I am profoundly convinced that Russian poetry *per se* has only one such pre-existing, stable vertical line of meaning, which I shall call its *topoi*. If not, then it is a somewhat limited selection of themes ("topoi") on which every important Russian poet feels almost obliged to speak—directly or indirectly, and sometimes unconsciously, which just goes to show that these topoi are *already there*. Their line-up is *roughly* as follows:

swimmer or *sailor* (sail, sailboat, Baratynsky's "steamship");
singer;
poet and crowd;
prophet;
bird;
genius (Zhukovsky's "pure genius of beauty", Pushkin's "genius of pure
    beauty", but also Zhukovsky's, Batyushkov's and Tsvetaeva's
    "my genius" in the Roman sense of the word);

dressing-gown (penates, home: Prince Vyazemsky, Batyushkov);
goblet; dagger (Vysotsky's "black pistol");
railroad station:
ring;
chariot of life;
road (from Lermontov's famous "I come out alone on to the road"
    (1841) to Tiutchev's "Now I wander on the high road" (1864)
    to Sosnora's "I come out alone. There is no road" (late 1970s);
    and last but not least:
monument.

All these "topoi" have their special dynamics of expansion (which I have not observed in the poetry of other countries); for instance, Lermontov's lone sail of 1832 (an anthology piece, but springing from the "swimmers/sailors" of Zhukovsky, Yazykov and Pushkin's "Arion" of 1827) is gradually transformed into Gumilyov's "lost tram" (1920) and 25 years before this Balmont's alliterative incantation ("Black boat beyond black art", 1894)—much abused for "formalism" or "absurdism" by critics who didn't see that, like a pianist, Balmont was playing variations on an eternal Russian theme.

This tradition ("vertical line") came into existence in Russia in the 18th Century, developed in the 19th and remained unbroken into our modernity. It would be impossible to describe it fully here, even for just one topos, though this may be done in the future.

II.

One of the essential topoi, one of the most loved, best known, most studied, most read. etc. etc., is of course the *monument*. As we know, in contradistinction to the others I have listed, this is a borrowed topos. It came into being in eighteenth-century Russia, rising like a phoenix from Roman ash (and like a phoenix it will continue to be reborn) in the transposition by Mikaelo Lomonosov of Horace's famous *Exegi monumentum* which is printed above.

The critic L. A. Musorina has said of this "translation" and of the whole topos of the monument in Russian poetry that it is founded on a misreading, in that Lomonosov, writing of "everywhere" and the "fatherland" apparently understood the river Aufidus and king Davnus as belonging to different parts of the Roman empire, whereas both are situated in Apulia, where Horace was born. As a result, the writers who came after Lomonosov, such as Derzhavin and Pushkin, saw the poet's fame spread across the whole width of the Russian empire. If indeed Lomonosov's translation was "incorrect" and gave rise to a whole series of "incorrect" transpositions—a comedy of errors—then we must accept (a) that this topos in Russia was due to a very *fruitful* mistake in Lomonosov and that his whole poem is not so much a translation as a transposition; (b) that this topos is thus only apparently based on translation, but is in reality "influenced but independent" from Derzhavin to the present. Horace was, therefore only a jumping-off point for a Russian tradition which would run another 267 years.

One further point on this "incorrect" translation. The critic for some reason *forgot* that the first "variation" on Horace was written—in Rome—by Ovid at the conclusion of his *Metamorphoses*:

> My work is complete: a work which neither Jove's anger, nor fire nor sword shall destroy, nor yet the gnawing tooth of time. That day which has power over nothing but my body may, when it pleases, put an end to my uncertain span of years. Yet with my better part I shall soar, undying, far above the stars, and my name will be imperishable. Wherever Roman power extends over the lands Rome has subdued, people will read my verse. If there be truth in poets' prophecies, I shall live to all eternity, immortalized by fame.   [tr. Mary M. Innes]

It is far from impossible that the highly educated Lomonosov deliberately wove into his Horatian poem some lines from Ovid (in italic above).

Let us also note that there is no "monument" in Lomonosov's poem, only the circumlocutory "mark of immortality". And if he translated *in this way*, replacing the "monument" with the euphemistic "mark of immortality" (a brilliant approximation, seeming to feel its way to the object and its meaning), this was no doubt deliberate, since he could have expressed himself more directly, like Horace. Why then did Derzhavin—"ignorant of Latin"—bring the word "monument" back into his so-called translation, if he (and after him Pushkin and Batyushkov) did indeed "borrow" everything, including their vocabulary, from Lomonosov? Lomonosov's transposition (note that he doesn't say a word about *himself*) is rather a record of personal experience in relation to Horace's poem, and the power of *such* a quality of verbal experience was passed on, like a relay baton, from Lomonosov to Derzhavin, and then to Batyushkov and Pushkin, and so on…. And the longer this relay lasted, the further each successive poem was from Horace and the closer (both in its vocabulary and its distortions) to some other Russian text (see for instance the parodic versions of Derzhavin's text in Voznesensky's "Perhaps" (1970) and Parshchikov's "Village Churchyard" (2004).

III.

There are "variations" on the *monument* theme in English and American poetry too, but of a different kind, not confined to Horace's poem, but taking from it *ideas* about the victory of poetry over the man-made monuments of time. We find this in Shakespeare's sonnets ("Not marble, nor the gilded monuments", Sonnet 55) and in Pope's "Rape of the Lock" ("And Monuments, like Men, submit to Fate!"). And nearer to us there is a brilliant remaking of Horace's poem by Ezra Pound:

This monument will outlast metal and I made it
More durable than the king's seat, higher than pyramids.
Gnaw of the wind and rain?

                     Impotent
The flow of years to break it, however many.

But let us return to the three Russian monuments of Derzhavin, Pushkin and Batyushkov. We can draw up a list, first of *what* Horace sees as his merits as a poet, and then of *what*—what *future* and *why*— the other poets foresee for themselves (taking it for granted that their *monuments* are separate poetic creations, though they pay tribute to a common topos). In Horace, it goes as follows:

1. I have completed a monument that is longer-lasting than bronze and higher than royal pyramids—one that corrosive rain and the uncontrollable north wind will never destroy, nor the endless sequence of years nor the flight of Time
2. I shall not wholly die, the greater part of me will escape from the goddess of Death: I shall grow ever higher, thanks to the praise of posterity, as long as
   a) the high priest climbs up to the Capitol with the silent Vestal Virgin
   b) they continue to speak of me where the wild Aufidus roars and where Daunus ruled over a rustic people, as of one who,
   c) rising from the depths to the heights of fame, became
   d) the one who first set the songs of Aeolia to the tunes of Italy (i.e. who adapted Greek meters to Latin).
3. Receive, Melpomene, what you have genuinely deserved, and condescend to wreathe my hair with Delphic laurel.

IV.

In Derzhavin (1795), we find:

1. The same as in Horace, but with an essential addition: the monument is defined and named: *miraculous, eternal;*
2. All as in Horace, but with a vital addition, Derzhavin's signature mark at the beginning of the line: *So!* With these exclamation marks, already used by him in the ode on the death of Prince Meshchersky (the founding text in the genre of Russian elegies on death) and clashing out like cymbals in an orchestra (think of Hitchcock's *The Man Who Knew Too Much*), and sometimes even in the middle of a line, Derzhavin indicated as with marks on a music score the intonation of a poem. And we should not forget that to Russian ears, this *tak*, with an exclamation mark, sounds almost like the Latin *sic!*;

   a) *Nothing from Horace,* but Derzhavin offers an explanation for his eternal fame that is overwhelmingly brilliant (in both its phonetic and historiosophical power): *While still the Slavs are honoured here on earth,* i.e. until all the Slavs have died out, I too, Derzhavin, shall be eternal: wow!

   b) then Derzhavin sets out the geographical boundaries (they are "boundless") of his future (i.e. eternal) fame: from the White Sea in the North to the Black Sea in the South (what else was to be expected from the friend of Crimean Potemkin?) to the Neva in the West, to the Ural in the East; there is not just a map of 18th Century Russia here, but the metaphor of a compass;

   c) Almost as in Horace, but with a new slant—"the peoples' songs" (**in Russian "innumerable peoples"**) will not forget him);

d) further explanation, more extensive than in Horace—and naturally, Lomonosov—of why he will be remembered, 1) for what can be called the ironic audacity of 2) the ode "Felitsa" dedicated to Catherine the Great, where he writes (in a pedagogic tone) of the "virtues" needed by sovereigns; 3) for the ode "God" and the *tone* of this ode, its "simple words", i.e. the tone of conversation; 4) for always saying what he thinks ("the truth") to tsars, even if smilingly (more or less a repetition of 2);

3. The same, or nearly the same, as in Horace, except that the Muse becomes the poet himself (his face, and not something *above* him, as in Horace).

V.

And now Pushkin (1836, published 1841):

1. *Nothing from Horace!* Like Derzhavin, Pushkin has *built himself* a monument, but Derzhavin's two adjectives are replaced by a single one "not made by hands" (*nerukotvornyi*). Then "the people" appear (**in Russian "the people's path"**), in contrast with Derzhavin's "innumerable peoples". This concept or term "people" (*narod*)—i.e. a *single* Russian people—was elaborated by the historian Karamzin (*History of the Russian People*) and the subsequent Romantic movement in Russia; in the 18th Century, i.e. *before* Romanticism, the *people* was given a variety of names: Russia, *Rossy*, the Russian state (*derzhava*—in this context the name Derzhavin seemed representative), or finally, simply the Slavs—but not one people (entity-and-unity). Incidentally, Napoleon (not only a child of the French Revolution, but the greatest *Romantic hero* of the period) was officially known as the

Emperor not of France (the territory) but of the French (the people). Instead of "pyramids" and "metals", which the poet's monument outdoes in "longlastingness" and "stability", Pushkin, *for the first time* in the history of this topos, finds a suitable architectural feature in his own time against which to measure his height and come out on top: Alexander's column—a column standing opposite the Winter Palace in St Petersburg, on the summit of which stands a baby-faced angel resembling Alexander I, erected after the Russian victories over Napoleon. In choosing this *object*, the ne'er-do-well Pushkin "went to extremes" (for the *first*, but not the last time in his *monument*), since this makes it appear that his, Pushkin's, literary victories are higher (i.e. more longlasting, in every respect) *even* than the great victory over Napoleon and its leader, the Russian tsar. To make *such* a claim then was like writing in the Stalinist years (something that never happened, of course) that "my" monument is higher than either the Mausoleum (not difficult in principle, but symbolically unthinkable, sacrilegious), or the buildings of Moscow University (one of Stalin's towers, and a bulwark of Soviet architecture); or, today, that it surpasses victory in the Great Fatherland War.

2. *The extremes continue!* How long will I, Pushkin be remembered? Answer: "as long as in this world there is *a single* poet living", i.e. as long as *just one man on earth* writes poetry, I, Pushkin, am immortal! One may not want to imagine it, but it is conceivable that all Derzhavin's "Slavs" might either die out or lose all sense of their race, like the Lombards or the Huns. But it is *absolutely* impossible to imagine—even after an "atomic winter", an Armageddon, or an alien invasion—that not a single person would be left to whisper a few lines (writing is not essential, and this would not be prose, which is indeed written speech, and not oral, mnemonic).

In other words, Pushkin's great gesture here is not local in character, or even utopian/universal, but in the highest degree existential!

a) Where Derzhavin gives the compass points of Russia, Pushkin speaks of peoples and their languages (their individual languages and not the Russian language unifying them): "in every language spoken by...". It is interesting that Pushkin doesn't write here of his poems as such, but of his "name", or rather of the *mythology* of that name ("I shall be spoken of"). That is to say that this name will be known to *all*, correctly pronounced in their own languages;

b) Pushkin then follows Derzhavin (and to a certain extent Horace) in listing what he considers his poetic achievements. But in Pushkin it is not particular poems that survive (as is suggested by Derzhavin), and not the poems in general (their "style" or, as in Horace, Greek prosody), but only the *feelings* they awaken ("with my lyre I stirred their tender feelings"). (Zhukovsky, when he was trying after Pushkin's death to get the "monument" poem through Nicholas I's censorship, changed "tender feelings" (*chuvstva dobrye*) to "alert feelings" (*chuvstva bodrye*)—Nicholas valued alertness and a military bearing, which is why he didn't notice Pushkin's seditious self-importance in the preceding stanzas; and in any case Alexander's column had a stiff military bearing, didn't it?). However, the memory of these feelings (as against the name) is not eternal according to Pushkin, but merely *long-lasting* ("I shall long be loved") although in Russian it would have been possible to write "eternal" and keep to the same metrical pattern. Two other feelings are mentioned: freedom and "charity for the defeated" (for the Decembrists, of course, but also New Testament charity)—that's all. It's for us to decide if this is a self-deprecation beyond pride, or on the contrary an extraordinary clarity of mind in someone who knows already that any poems (even the greatest) will inevitably sink (like a stone in water) with the ripples fading out into nothing, and that once the circles are gone only one thing will remain, the name, not the "reputation" but merely the sound.

3. *Nothing* here from Horace or Derzhavin apart from the mention of the muse; neither the laurel wreath, nor the "dawn" of immortality with which the muse crowns them. In Pushkin there seems to be a sudden diminuendo (as against their *apotheosis*)—or rather it seems that the extremism (both in image and emotion) of the first three stanzas is toned down in the fourth with its broader understanding and sinks in this final stanza to a (remarkable) *selfless* sadness (meaning that it is no doubt *sad* to recognize such things, but what can be done about it?). Pushkin asks "his" muse for four things: a) to obey *only* the voice from above ("the will of God", which is something different from the usual Romantic "inspiration", since the criterion here is *ethical*); 2) to fear no-one and nothing (except God), and not to ask for "honour" (**a wreath in Russian**—this *gesture* of renunciation of worldly rewards goes against what we find in Horace and Derzhavin); 3) to respond equally ironically—or not at all, Pushkin writes "indifferently", which is the same thing—to blame and praise (otherwise you would not be able to prevent yourself collapsing or burning up); 4) never to quarrel with idiots ("fools"). In general terms, Pushkin is proposing here a quite new model of behaviour for the poet, and not only the Romantic poet. It is far from the familiar romantic model (whereby the poet was, as Pushkin put it, compelled to seek refuge "by the shore of lonely waters, among broad-rustling oaks"), but a *humanly* pragmatic model—*don't* fuss, *don't* expect ("demand") anything,

don't do anything—this being (apart from obeying God) a very gentle "don't do" in place of the imperative "do". Pushkin's "don't expect" (later reincarnated in Bulgakov's "never ask for anything") doesn't at all mean "don't hope", since it is hope, and the poetic certainty that it exists in human language, that fills the first stanzas of Pushkin's *monument.*

VI.

Konstantin Batyushkov's version of the *monument* is also *absolutely* unique. The life of Batyushkov, the Russian Tasso or Hölderlin, was divided into two equal parts by what they call genetic madness. For his first 34 years (1787-1821), he was living, for the next 34 (1821-1855) it was as if he was *not* living ("I am no longer in this world", he wrote in a letter). When he was living, he wrote; when he was not living, he wrote nothing. But in 1826—suddenly!—he included in one of his letters a new poem, "Imitation of Horace", which was not printed until 1883 (his modern biographer, Anna Sergeeva-Klyatis, believes for some reason that the poem was written in 1849). In the academic Biblioteka Poeta edition of 1964, which I am using here, this poem was reproduced not in the main text, but in the notes, and described, for understandable (in this case Soviet) censorship reasons as a "nonsensical collection of phrases" (this was the time of the *fight against formalism,* "nonsense in place of music", etc., which they even managed to find in the 19th Century). All the signs are that Batyushkov himself saw this poem as something particularly important for himself, since he himself translated it into French prose.

The poem is not well known today; it is given in translation above. As we can see, it is more an imitation of *Derzhavin* than of Horace. It can be seen as the "poem of a madman" (as it has by D. Blagoy, the biographer A. Sergeeva-Klyatis, Academician M. Alekseev, and N. Fridman in the Biblioteka Poeta), but it is equally possible to attempt to understand the poem through Batyushkov's "own logic" (after all, illogicality, especially in poetry, is also a kind of logic). So:

1) The poem starts very much as in Derzhavin, but: "I have built a monument", not "built *myself* a monument" as in Derzhavin and Pushkin. The adjectives too are different: where Derzhavin has "miraculous, eternal", Batyushkov has "huge, miraculous". A "huge monument" sounded very strange in the 19th Century. If Derzhavin's "miraculous monument" refers to the notion of a miracle (a unique event, as in the Bible), Batyushkov's "miraculous" is one of surprise at the huge dimensions of the thing. And if the monument is not built for himself, who is it for? It turns out—and this is the first novelty for this topos—that it is for *other people* ("singing your praises)". Or perhaps one other person, since "you" could well refer to a single person who remains unidentified. It is possible that this "you", given Batyushkov's cosmopolitan culture, could echo the first line of Goethe's dedication of *Faust*: "You approach again, elusive figures". Batyushkov's monument "will not see death" precisely because he has honoured these *others*, who might also include Tasso, Ariosto, Parny; friends (he wrote many epistles to friends); military comrades; an earthly woman (or women); or maybe the bucolic shepherdesses of Arcadia or even Melchisedech himself (the subject of Batyushkov's last poem).

2) Now it is *I, Batyushkov* (and not it, the monument), who will not see death—"like your sweet image, charming, benevolent"... Again, Batyushkov does not put himself *above* the image of *her* or *them*, an eternal, undying image: "charming", incidentally, does not necessarily refer to a woman: remember the charming "baby face" of Aleksandr 1 (and Batyushkov took part in all the anti-Napoleonic campaigns, knew the tsar personally, though apparently he didn't like him). The parenthetic "Witness Napoleon, our faithful friend" is enigmatic, but only on first reading;

the fact that it is picked out in parentheses might suggest that to see Napoleon as bearing the responsibility (for he is a "witness") for Batyushkov's "immortality" is not only ironic, but also a coarse soldierly truth. Batyushkov fought against him and knows that Napoleon is not only the enemy, but the principal *Romantic hero* of his generation (think of Prince Andrey's Napoleon cult in *War and Peace*, or later on, after the event, the image of Napoleon on Saint Helena, the Romantic symbol of proud solitude and independence—as in Pushkin's "To the Sea" or Lermontov's "The Ship of the Air"). Napoleon is *ours*, a *friend.* When Batyushkov writes "our", he could not be referring to the Russian state (only the tsar could allow himself the imperial "we"). But this "our" sets Batyushkov's Romantics against Derzhavin's Slavs; Derzhavin would not die "while still the Slavs are honoured", and Batyushkov, while there is still a Romantic *nature* (nature, and not a literary movement).

3) It is not "my greater part" that will "dodge oblivion" in Batyushkov, but "all I have done in letters" (*vse moi tvoreniya*). It may seem to come to the same thing (the "greater part" is the poems), but not quite. In Batyushkov's poem, the verse will live not in posterity, but *in print*, i.e. though being reprinted! This is almost an anticipation of Walter Benjamin's "Age of Mechanical Reproduction" as a guarantee of immortality. Batyushkov *gambles* not on popular *memory* (the inevitably *grateful* memory of posterity), like all the other authors for this topos, but on the Gutenberg press. In other words, it is not books that are subject to decay, but *memory*—if the books are not reprinted.

4) Batyushkov's doctor (Dietrich) noted that he someties signed himself, whether seriously or in jest, Konstantin Bog (Konstantin God)—i.e. B...g *in place of* B...v. And there is in this poem a "suggestion" of arrogance: "Not

Phoebus, I alone..." But is it really arrogance? "These
fetters" is an allusion to Derzhavin's ode "God" where
the "chain of being" is borrowed from Pope's "Essay on
Man". Pope's chain stretches roughly speaking from the
mosquito to the angels and God, with man in the middle
(the "lock" that shuts the whole chain); this is the source
of Derzhavin's famous "I am a slave—I am a worm—I
am a tsar—I am God" (note the dashes, which seem to
visualize the chain)—is this perhaps where the signature
"Konstantin God" came from? In Batyushkov it is the poet
himself who "forges" this chain, and not the conventional
Phoebus or Apollo Musagetes, leader of the Muses, a
name beloved of the 18th and 19th Centuries. There is, of
course, a reference here not only to Derzhavin's *universe*,
but also to the last stanza in Horace and Derzhavin, where
the Muse rewards the poet. It follows that it is not the
Muse or Apollo Musagetes, who can evaluate the poet,
since he *himself* is responsible for the forging of his chain
(which Mandelstam, a great admirer of Batyushkov, called
tradition or a *seminar*). The poet, as Batyushkov sees it (and
in his *monument* he speaks only of poetry, not of peoples
and posterity), creates and follows his own tradition (his
vertical line) out of everything that has been and that is;
in other words he is his own Phoebus Apollo and the *lock*
on the chain.

5) The enumeration of his achievements is again semi-parodic
in relation to Derzhavin. The deviations or substitutions—
while the vocabulary remains almost entirely that of
Derzhavin—are significant in that everything else is
preserved. So the "virtue" or "worth" is no longer Felitsa's
(i.e. Catherine's) but Elise's, Elise being Batyushkov's
great-niece Elizaveta Grigorievna Grevens, for whom this
poem was indeed written. There may also be a reference
here to the French poet Parny, whom Batyushkov had
admired and translated, and whose lyrical heroine is

called Eléanore; the sound of this name suggests the French pronoun *elle*, so it and Elise may represent here all women, like Catullus' Lesbia or Propertius' Cynthia.

6) In what follows, Batyushkov does not address the Muse (why bother, since he himself is the Musagetes?), but the "tsars"—which is highly unusual for this topos. Or rather, he speaks, not to the tsars, but to the *tsaritsas* (once again to women, and in the imperative: "Be stars for us, my empress, my tsaritsas" (**note that the translation follows the sounds of *tsar* to the image of all-powerful stars: the literal meaning of the Russian is "Tsaritsas, rule, and you, the empress"**). There are several layers of meaning here. To address a woman as tsaritsa (empress) was a poetic convention at the time. The actual empress at the time (1826, not 1849) was Aleksandr I's widow, Elizaveta Alekseevna (another Elise). So the move from women/tsaritsas to a particular woman (the empress), is logical enough; they are links in one chain. And why not tsars? Why, because he, Batyushkov, is the tsar on Mount Pindus (yes, the mountain of Apollo and the muses). So to call Venus *sister*, if "you" are Apollo and were the first in Russia to sing of love with such force as Batyushkov did, is quite natural. But why "little sister"? Because Batyushkov's own sister was also called Elizaveta (Elise). Thus *Elise* is in principle the best eponym both for the French *elle*, and for Batyushkov himself (and the three women of the poem). In other words, all is clear and logical: let love rule the world, as I, Batyushkov, rule the muses!

7) But the most famous thing in this *monument* is the last line, which seems to herald Khlebnikov: *A kesar' moi—svyatoi kosar' (But my Caesar is the sacred reaper).* Note that the previous lines are not divided into stanzas, but that this last line is set out. In other words, this is a statement, and the whole line, with its striking word play, carries the greatest possible charge. If we read this line as a set of

allusions to the New Testament, it is clear that 'Caesar' is also the Russian tsar ("Render to Caesar the things that are Caesar's "), but in what way is he a tsar for Apollo/ Batyushkov? And the sacred reaper comes from Matthew's gospel (9. 37-38): "Then saith he unto his disciples, The harvest truly is plenteous, but the labourers are few; Pray ye therefore the Lord of the harvest, that he will send forth labourers into his harvest." These "labourers" (reapers)—the apostles, and ideally every Christian called on to complete God's harvest—are the emblem of a higher power for Batyushkov, and later for his "follower" Mandelstam, in whom we find the logical continuation of this "statement": "poetry is power". *In hoc signo vinces!*

[Translator's note: there is a contradiction between the highly persuasive interpretation given by Ilya Kutik and my own freer rendering of the final line, where following the bidding of the echoing words, "Caesar" gives rise to "scissors" and thus to a pagan image of Atropos, the oldest of the Fates cutting with her scissors "abhorred shears" the thread of life. Another kind of power...]

LUCIFER'S PALE PEARL:
ON THE POETRY OF SALVADOR DÍAZ MIRÓN

Anthony Seidman

The Mexican poet Salvador Díaz Mirón (1853-1928) led a violent, politically active, and aesthetically vibrant life that rivals the biographies of Lord Byron and Espronceda. Many of his poems were staple strophes recited at public events, memorized by school children, and clumsily imitated by lesser poets. Ironically, he officially recognized only one of his collections, *Lascas* (1901), compiled rather late in life and in his poetic development. Until then, his work was published widely in Latin America in periodicals and journals devoted to contemporary literature; the concept of a Latin American literature was then still considered groundbreaking, and the major voices of that period, such as Rubén Darío and José Martí, appeared in the same publications alongside Díaz Mirón. The early poems of Díaz Mirón were successful attempts at capturing the fading crepuscular glimmer of Spanish-language Romanticism, be it the suicidal melancholia of the Mexican Manuel Acuña, or the sentimentalism of Gaspar Núñez de Arce.

In order to assert themselves as more than littérateurs from the boondocks, the Latin American poets surrounding Díaz Mirón generated a hyper-Parnassian poetry later known as *Modernismo*. Ironically, there was little Spanish poetry of quality being written in the country that had once given birth to the sonnets of Quevedo, or the *Coplas* of Manrique. The Nicaraguan Rubén Darío's *Azul...* (1888), an exquisite collection of verses and prose poems trumpeted the arrival of swans, rubies, tigers and princesses as the new appurtenances of the poem written in Spanish, designating the Americas as *the* place where the language was being reinvigorated. Díaz Mirón contributed to these changes as well, though perhaps less decisively; however, when *Lascas* was finally published, its printing of 15,000 copies was quickly exhausted.

Lascas has remained in print ever since, and while many of his contemporaries have become unfashionable—mention Amado Nervo reverentially to a contemporary Mexican poet, and he or she will cackle madly and express serious doubts about your intelligence—Díaz Mirón is still deeply admired. His is a voice that purified, as if by fire, the Romantic excesses of the early 19th Century. He deftly incorporates the metrical innovations of the *Modernistas*, while eschewing much of their preciousness, and embraces the grotesque and violent—an attitude inspired by Baudelaire. By the time Jorge Cuesta and the *Contemporáneos* published their scandalous (both for its exclusions and inclusions) anthology of Mexican poetry entitled *Antología de la Poesía Mexican Moderna* (1928), Cuesta asserted that Díaz Mirón´s poetry served as a bridge between Romanticism, Parnassianism, and Symbolism. This astute observation from an *enfant enragé* of the new Mexican poetry constituted a positive and lasting reassessment of Díaz Mirón´s poetry.

Díaz Mirón´s personal life teemed with weapons, hunting, duels, political intrigue, imprisonment, exile, and public service representing his native state of Veracruz. At the age of twenty-five, as a result of one of his duels, he suffered permanent damage to his left arm; from that point on, he identified with Lord Byron and his clubfoot. Like many poets, he loved intensely, yet his love life was a torrid affair; he married in 1881, but his wife was not the true love of his life. When his true love married, he wrote a wicked epithalamium commemorating her union with another. The poem crackles with a malignance that reminds the reader of the best of Baudelaire, especially of such poems as *A Celle Qui Este Trop Gaie*. Díaz Mirón writes:

There's no syrup, no fragrance
like your chatter...
what perfumed and
sugary lozenge will dissolve
its honey and ambergris
in your mouth,
O virgin!, when you
speak with me alone?
[...]
Your wedding-feast
is held tomorrow.
[...]
Could the sordid Earth,
a globe yoked
and dragged through
the fathomless void,
halt in its rounds,
then disintegrate
into nimbi
of tenuous gas...
[...]
Your wedding-feast
is held tomorrow.
[...]
O Tirsa! The hour has struck.
I lack all courage;
by the warbling of a lark,
I abandon my soul.
Dawn stirs awake and
smooths its pearly veil,
and Lucifer reveals
his pale pearl.

Other poems include deliciously grotesque depictions of public hangings, beggars, giant women, tropical landscapes, and the moribund. One can assume that these descriptions were more than schoolboy fancies. Díaz Mirón was the Caravaggio of Mexican poetry; he killed more than one man when he felt his honor was slighted. Other poems, such as *Cleopatra*, prove redolent of the Orientalism fashionable at the time; the poem conveys a sensuality that evokes an odalisque by Ingres:

> I espied her: naked, stretched
> atop purple sheets.
> Through a long
> pipe encrusted with diamonds
> and pearls, she inhaled
> extract of spices. Her head
>
> lay atop her left hand,
> and crowning her
> thick tresses, an opal
> diadem glistened
> like a tiger's gaze,
> blood-thirsty & blazing.
> [...]
> Her flesh was hot,
> and her breasts were like
> milk poured into chalices
> which turned into alabaster,
> firm, yet quivering.

The poem below is from Díaz Mirón's later poetry. The Romantic tone has been replaced by something that is undeniably modern. One thinks of the more lurid passages in *Les Chants de Maldoror* or *Les Fleurs du Mal*. The poem has been translated once or twice into English, most notably by Samuel Beckett, in the anthology of Mexican poetry edited by Octavio Paz. In my rendition I have strayed from the sonnet structure, seeking to preserve the energy of the original's syntax and to accentuate the bracing effect of its imagery.

MADE AN EXAMPLE

The bare corpse putrefying from the bough,
a grotesque fruit
still dangling from its stem,
proof of the severe verdict,
and rocking from its axis like a pendulum.

Glaring exposure of skin, tongue
jutting from the teeth's grimace,
and cowlick like a cock's comb,
rendered him a buffoon;
loafing near my saddle,
some beggars all rags & toothless gums
laughed, pointed.

And the solemn disposal, the tumid
overripe head
wafting a stench from the green branch
and smoldering to the solemn sway

of the incense holder,
while the sun arose through fleckless azure,
and the fields,—
some trope pilfered from Tibullus.

"O Captain, my Captain, my Captain!": Juan Parra del Riego's "Walt Whitman"

David Shook

Juan Parra del Riego (1894-1925) was born in Peru but spent the most productive years of his adult life in Uruguay. His early work exemplified Modernist tendencies, but before his premature death he had begun to explore early twentieth-century avant-garde techniques, primarily influenced by the Futurists. As a young poet in Lima, he was the first of the capital's literati to herald the work of César Vallejo, who at that time was based in Trujillo, in Northern Peru. In 1916 the poet moved to Paris, where he stayed with his friend Jules Supervielle. It was during his time in Europe that he began to display the first symptoms of the tuberculosis that would eventually kill him at the age of 31. Parra del Riego returned to Montevideo, Uruguay in 1921, where he vigorously promoted the new aesthetics he had encountered in Europe, composing four books of poetry and many popular poems about Uruguayan soccer before his death, five days after his wife, the Uruguayan poet Blanca Luz Brum, gave birth to their son.

This poem, Parra del Riego's tribute to Walt Whitman, demonstrates the naturalness with which Whitman's poetry works in Spanish. Parra del Riego includes famous lines like "O Captain, my Captain," which he has strangely appended, in the relentless enthusiasm of the poem, with another "my Captain," as well as unclear or polyreferential phrases involving Whitmanesque yells, candles of Curiosity, and wild, mystic harps. Throughout the poem the European avant-gardes occasionally raise their head—despite his beard, it is difficult to imagine Whitman on a motorcycle, and the poet's eagerness to leave everything behind strikes this translator as more Breton than Emerson. This poem was written at least ten years before the Nicaraguan Vanguardia's interest in his work, piqued by José Coronel Urtecho's travels to San Francisco, and, like their interest in his work, which manifests itself less obviously in the character of their compositions than in their general aesthetic principles, suggests a more complex relationship between Whitman and Latin American literature than Borges's oft-cited poem and the much alleged but seldom noticeable influence of Whitman on Neruda's work. Whitman's radical independence and self-expression appeals to Parra del Riego—as it did to the notably anti-*yanqui* Nicaraguans—as an emblematic feature of what it means to be American, a category in which they most definitely included themselves.

WALT WHITMAN

At the seaside I fire off this shout of colors
greeting and departure
of my soul with your soul, Walt Whitman!

I know how to swim! I know how to row!
I know how to sing! I know how to ride a horse!
My revolver has twelve shots
and my motorcycle is joyful like the sun.

I am the one that has run,
with a heart crazed with confidence,
to fraternize down every path with men.
I am a friend of acrobats,
of typographers, of the ill, of peasants and boxers.

I am the one able, all of a sudden,
to throw it all behind me, books, family, love, home and friends,
only for the virile pleasure
of testing my heart
with other lonely and dramatic days.

Oh, beloved Walt Whitman!
Freewill! Vigor! Joy!
I am the one that has run through every city
shouting, crazed with hope,
the new health of your pure songs
at poor poets without strength and without light!
Your songs touched by the hand of heaven and earth!
Your immortal songs made of mortal dreams!
Because you alone were the wild and mystic harp
that made my life clear freshness again
with the music of your remote geographies;
and at night I was filled by strange and longing
schemes of purity, of perfection and strength.

When I read you it looked like I had returned from the countryside.
In my heart the candles of Curiosity, of Energy and Enthusiasm
were raised high, swift and joyful.
You alone were the one that heated the course of my passion,
this violent will to travel,
this ardor, this love for heroes,
for the freedom and the personality
that is the wide altar of my pathways,
where stubbornly pure and solitary
I die and burn,
I burn and rise,
I rise!
Walt Whitman!

Up with the souls!
The cavalry, the music
the gardens, the flowers, the sea, and the women!
Four hundred swimmers on the wave of a tenacious, joyful head!

The blaze! The dramatic station with the departure of the trains!
What is above the Southern Cross
and what is beneath the fantastic eyelids of the mad.
The total symphony of earth and life!
The son of God that came with his songs of strength and hope!

That was you Walt Whitman!
The perfect comrade! The Revelator!
Our grand fountain of strength, Americans!

Oh, beloved Walt Whitman!
O Captain, my Captain, my Captain!
More than all the philosophers
you taught me strength and nobility,
with your agile, sky-blue eyes
and your face of aurora
on the smoke of your beard like a natural saint's.

O Captain, my Captain, my Captain!
You say: everything returns.
But against your chest I yell:
nothing returns!
Strength is continuing crazed with confidence until the end!
with our hearts sonorous like thunderbolts
marching onward without cease.

THE POEMS OF INNOKENTY ANNENSKY

Peter France

The outstanding Russian modernist poet Gennady Aygi once told a Yugoslav interviewer: "Suddenly, reaching the age of fifty, it turns out that the two Russian poets who have remained most necessary and closest to me are Lermontov and Innokenty Annensky." And about Annensky, he explained: "Annensky, in my opinion, could be called the first "existential" poet in the history of European poetry" (Gennady Aygi, *Field-Russia*, New York: New Directions, 2007, pp. 19-20).

Innokenty Fedorovich Annensky was born in Omsk in 1855, the son of a civil servant. The family returned in 1860 to St Petersburg, where Annensky attended school and university, graduating in classical languages. His childhood and youth were marked by frequent illness and by his father's financial troubles and forced retirement. He taught Latin and Greek in schools in the capital and in Kiev, becoming headmaster of the prestigious "lycée" at Tsarskoe Selo. He was only just beginning to be appreciated as a poet at the time of his death, from heart failure, in 1909.

Annensky was neglected as a poet during his life-time and belonged to no literary groupings. He is sometimes associated with his contemporaries, the Symbolists, but does not really belong with them, even though he admired and translated Mallarmé. Since his death, however, he has had a body of devoted followers in Russia, beginning with Nikolay Gumilyov and Anna Akhmatova. On the other hand, it is still true, as Dimitri Obolensky remarked in his 1962 *Penguin Book of Russian Verse*, that the "flawless beauty [of his poetry] has not been sufficiently appreciated outside Russia." Whether a translator should attempt to convey "flawless beauty" is debatable, but Annensky's distinctive voice is one that ought to be heard, even through the medium of English.

Some idea of what that voice is can be gained from Osip
Mandelstam's remarks about Annensky's translations of Euripides (this
complete Russian Euripides is one of the outstanding monuments
of Russian translation): "he absorbed the serpentine venom of wise
Hellenic speech, preparing a brew of such bitter wormwood-strong
verses as have never been written before or since." Apart from four
classical tragedies of his own and some remarkable critical essays, his
work consists entirely of short lyric poems, dense and sharp in their
diction, attentive both to the sensations of life and to the shifts of an
acute and tormented sensibility.

Some of his best poems are gathered in his posthumous collection
The Cypress Casket (so named from the wooden box in which he kept
them). Many are arranged in groups of three, so-called "trefoils," often
with rather arbitrary titles and apparently grouped on a principle of
contrast and variety. Four of these trefoils are given in their entirety
here. They are followed by a group of free-standing poems, including
a famous address to St Petersburg. "To a Sister" is addressed not to the
poet's sister, but to his sister-in-law, the wife of his elder brother, who
with her husband gave him a place of refuge in his troubled adolescence.

The poem "Balloons for the Kids" is an original notation of street
patter, reminding one perhaps of Petrushka and prefiguring similar
ventures such as Blok's "The Twelve." My attempt to translate it is a
bit of a free-wheeling experiment, more concerned with rhyme and
rhythm than with literal meaning.

Innokenty Annensky
translated from the Russian by
Peter France

TREFOIL OF TEMPTATION: POPPIES

Cheerful day is burning... Among drowsy grasses
Poppies make stains—like greedy weakness,
Like lips that are full of temptation and poison,
Like scarlet butterflies' wide-open wings.

Cheerful day is burning... But the garden lies empty.
Long ago it finished with temptation and feasting,—
And under the shade of heaven's radiant chalice.
Lie withered poppies, like old women's heads.

TREFOIL OF TEMPTATION: BOW AND STRINGS

What heavy, dark delirium!
Those moonlit-turbid heights!
To touch the violin so many years
And not know the strings in the light!

Who needs us? And who lit up
Two yellow, two gloomy faces?...
Suddenly the bow felt someone
Pick them up and merge them.

"How long ago! But through the gloom
Tell me one thing: is it you?"
And the strings nestled close to him,
Sounding, but trembling too.

"Is it really true, never again
Shall we part? Could we wish for more?"
And the violin was answering *yes*,
But the violin's heart was sore.

The bow understood it all, fell silent,
But the violin echoed still...
And what was music to those who listened
Was torture to those two.

But the man did not blow out the flame
Till daybreak...The strings sang on...
And the sun found them lying there
On black velvet, their strength all gone.

Innokenty Annensky, trans. Peter France

TREFOIL OF TEMPTATION: IN MARCH

Let it go, the nightingale in the sweet flowers,
But never forget the *morning* of love!
And the bright black breast of the waking earth
          In the still unawakened leaves!

Under the scraps of its snowy blouse
Only once did it know desire,—
Only once did it drink of fiery March
          More drunk than with wine!

Only once we could not tear envious eyes
From the newly swollen earth,
Only once we entwined our frigid hands
And trembling hurried out of the garden…
          Only once… that once…

Innokenty Annensky, trans. Peter France

LUNAR TREFOIL: WINTER SKY

Down and away flew the melting snow,
Cheeks burned red and glistened.
I had not thought the moon was so small
Or the clouds so smokily distant.

Asking for nothing, I'll go away,
For my number is up, for ever.
I had not thought the moon was so fair
Or so fearful up in heaven.

Midnight is near. No-one, no-one's,
Worn out by the spectre of life,
I marvel at the moonbeams' smoke
In my treacherous fatherland.

LUNAR TREFOIL: MOONLIT NIGHT AT WINTER'S END

We are at the station,
By night forgotten,
Moonlit night so quiet
In the forest clearing...
Do I dream—or truly
Are we at the station
By night forgotten?

You came from afar,
Exhausted engine!
Boards—pallid yellow,
Silver-and-yellow,
And the dead frost melting
Clings to the rail track.
Have you come where you meant,
Exhausted engine?
Quiet in the moonlight,
Or are they a vision,
These shadows and the weary
Sighing of the engine,
And all painted silver
By the pearly moonlight,
The swarthy, lanky
Station guard who carries
His unneeded lantern
Over patterned shadows?

Innokenty Annensky, trans. Peter France

Din-din-din—it passes,
Beyond this vision
That is left unfinished
So irretrievably,
So irremediably,
Somewhere still ringing,
Just barely audible...

29 March 1906, on the Vologda-Totma highway

LUNAR TREFOIL: TRÄUMEREI

Was it only the shades that had gathered,
Only shades in a May night of moonlight?
Or the lights or the flowers of lilac
Shining white and down on your knees there
    Gently falling?
Did I really, unreasoning, love you
    Unthinking
In May's languid shadows?
    Bending down to the flowers of lilac
On that night, on that May night of moonlight,
    Did I kiss your knees there
Clasping them and unclasping,
In the languid, the languid May shadows?
Or was it a vision, the garden,
On that night, on that May night of moonlight,
Or perhaps I am just a mute shadow?
Or are you just my suffering,
    Beloved,
Since for us there can be no meeting
In the night, in the May night of moonlight...

Night, May 6-7 1906, on the Vologda train

Innokenty Annensky, trans. Peter France

FAIRGROUND TREFOIL: SILVER NOON

The gleam of silver at noon
Has not yet scattered the mist,
Shot through with wounds of the sun
The mist is still yellower at noon,
Still yellower, still more deathly.
But noon is burning so sternly
That now I can barely endure
The snatches of lilac and scarlet
Of balloons that the eye just makes out
Among scraps of funereal fire.
And why should they all come running,
These joyful, these crazy crowds
Seeking to capture the sun?
And why should the sun caress them,
Airy creatures in a dead space!
But in incense all will grow dim,
The silver of flames and brocade,
The pomp of the undertaker:
For Pierrot and Harlequin
Come with candles to stand at the grave!
Oh white funereal pomp!

FAIRGROUND TREFOIL: BALLOONS FOR THE KIDS

Balloons, come and buy my balloons!
Balloons from the kids!
Money from the dads!
Young gents, come and buy my balloons!
Foxy coat, let's see your spare cash,
Don't cling on to the trash:
I'll let them fly up to the sky,
In two hours, look out, look up high!
It's good to be free, so they say.
Tweet-tweet, your worship, let's play.
Just buy, they'll be on cloud nine.
No bargaining—three seventy-five!
     Could I take any less
     For emancipation—bliss?
     No, you won't....
Hey Granny, what d'you want?
     Just a tot?
Sorry, but see what I've got....
     So it goes—
Another one grows,
But our Punch
with his head screwed on tight
doesn't grow a fat paunch,
but looks high in the sky
with his lofty thoughts.
Which one will you have?
Don't squeeze me until I am yours,
Mess it up and it's flat...
     Balloons for the kids,
     Red ones, purple ones,
     Cheap as they come!
     Balloons for the kids!

Hey, fur collar, speak Fritz?
Take ten—they're in couples
And the rest for free...
Shame your German's so weak,
Talk's better than roubles!
Let's have you, old man!
It's like you—spick and span—
This great big fatty,
      Yellow as putty,
With a heart saying Katy...
      Going for a song
      Just five,
And another twenty-five,
And then ten more for the best.
Here's one with the government crest!
      Balloons, buy my kiddies' balloons!
      Good people, just buy my balloons,
      And then you watch out, you saloons!

Innokenty Annensky, trans. Peter France

FAIRGROUND TREFOIL: DYING

Thank God, here is the shade again!
Why it is I do not know,
But since the morning I have felt
This dying hanging over me
All the livelong twilit day!
Serving out its bitter time
Between decrepit yellow walls,
Shrivelled , shuddering on its string,
A gloomy red balloon hangs there
Between decrepit yellow walls!
And impotent, just like a shade,
All this livelong twilit day
Keeps tugging, tugging at the string,
Unable to cut short its pain
All this livelong twilit day…
If only night came quickly, night!
To feel yourself slipping away
Into swooning, reconciled
And stupefied, going out again
Into the stupefying night!
And if up there above my head
That dark red thing, barely alive
Would wait its time over the bed
Before becoming so like me…
That dark thing, barely alive,
Up there, right above my head…

Innokenty Annensky, trans. Peter France

TREFOIL OF FIRE: AMETHYSTS

When, burning away the colour blue,
The crimson day grows furiously,
How often I invoke the dusk,
The chilly dusk of amethysts.

Not so that the day's torrid rays
Should burn facets of amethyst,
But that the candle's glimmering
Should flow like water, fierily,

And splintering in violet shards,
The shining there confirm the sense
That somewhere we feel no binding cords,
But a resplendent confluence.

TREFOIL OF FIRE: DOVE-GREY SUNSET

Dove-grey sunset came near,
The air was heady, tender,
And a special shade of green
Somehow filled the shadowed garden.

And proclaiming the Unseen one
In clouds of melting sorrow,
In the air so full of rain
Trumpets gently sounded.

Then, like a vivid call
In the distance, an explosion:
Piercing the gentle clouds,
A copper sun was laughing.

Innokenty Annensky, trans. Peter France

TREFOIL OF FIRE: JANUARY STORY

A crutch thumped steadily...
My last, my new year story,
Is that your voice I hear?

Lips didn't pray for happiness,
The room was deep in shade,
Lilies' wide-open chalices
Breathed grief of another place.

Caressing our dulled vision,
Flowers spoke in grief:
"We are what we have been
And will be, for ever... and you?"

Be silent...Is it not better
To daydream by the fire?...
The January sun not burning,
Its crystals so intense...

TO A SISTER

To A. N. Annenskaya

Evening—and the green nursery
With its low ceiling.
A boring book in German.
Nanny in glasses knitting.

I seem to see a novel,
A yellow paper-back…
I could even read the title
If this mist was less thick.

You were still Alina then,
A rosy thought in your eyes,
The big cape on your dress,
A grey shawl on your shoulders.

My knees deep in the chair
As I fixed my eyes on you,
I loved your tender hands
With their delicate veins.

The obscure flow of your words
Was my music of the spheres…
Where I listened for the clash
Of your own special r's…

In the bronze candlestick
A tallow candle gutters…
Sweet, quietly-sorrowful,
This all lives in the heart…

Innokenty Annensky, trans. Peter France

BLUE LONGING

Each day more, in warmth and beauty,
Ethereal space is overshadowed
By a sun-drained empty chalice:
Now like azure, now like sapphire.

Solar pavilions stand proudly
Flaming in the tender blueness,
And jealously the tufts of cotton
Cling to the sapphire, white and cloudy.

Take them, sun, they suffocate me—
Precious stones grow ever duller—
I desire the airy summits
Ever more crystalline and cooler,

Or better still, the dove-grey storm cloud
Subtly shifting, seeming water,
Dark apparelled , swarthy features,
Like the heart, tearful and heavy.

PETERSBURG

Yellow vapour of Petersburg winters,
Yellow snow, a blanket over the town;
I cannot tell how "we" and "you" differ—
I only know we are fused into one.

Were we concocted on a tsar's orders?
Or did the Swedes just leave us undrowned?
The past has left us nothing of legend,
Only the fearful facts and the stone.

Only the stone the magician left us,
And the Neva, all yellowy-brown,
And the dumb squares, stretching out like deserts,
Where they used to execute men before dawn.

But all that was ours when we lived in the city,
Urging the two-headed eagle of fame,
The cliff-top giant in the dark convents—
Tomorrow will be a children's game.

However he acted, fiercely, boldly,
Spurring on his furious horse,
The tsar could not crush to death the serpent—
It became the idol of later years.

No castles, no miracles, and no temples,
Hallucinations, nor tears, nor smiles,
Only the stone of the frozen deserts,
The fateful error that fills our minds.

Innokenty Annensky, trans. Peter France

Even in May when we can imagine
Wafting on the waters, the shades of white nights,
We see not dreams of spring with her magic,
We see the poison of barren desires.

"If it could be oblivion, not death…"

If it could be oblivion, not death,
Nothing to feel or hear or see...
For if you listen to my life,
It's not a life, but agony.

Do I not dwindle with you, days,
And wither with the maple leaves?
And do my flames not die away
Into the molten crystal's tears?

Am I not all in the solitude
Of cliffs, the birch trees' poverty?
Or in the roses' snowy fluff,
Gripped by the cold of the new day?

Or in the raindrops, hanging there,
Waiting like pearls to fall to earth?...
But tell me, in the pangs of thought
Is there a sympathetic heart?

On Translating Annensky's
"Anguish of Remembrance"

Robert Isaf

William Carlos Williams famously calls poems machines made out of words, and while I find great fault in the image I have to agree that considering poetry a matter of engineering comes with its advantages.

When working to translate a poem, I find that the original becomes a blueprint for itself, with my job being to re-create that original, following the specifications of the blueprint as exactly as possible, only in a wholly unsuitable material. Knowing that perfection is impossible, the most important question, the decision which determines whether a translation is successful or not, becomes: which elements of the blueprint are to be ignored, and to what extent? Or, asked another way; which element of the blueprint is most essential, and must be replicated correctly even at the expense of other elements?

The trouble with Annensky in general is that his blueprints are both simple and precise. Every element serves a purpose; and the original material (that is to say, the Russian language) is used elegantly, in constructions that take advantage of its natural strengths. Really that's part of what every poet strives for; Annensky simply pulls it off with a degree more simplicity and precision than is often the case. It's very good engineering.

For instance, we note one element in a poem's rhythm. In this case there's a regular meter, namely three anapests per line and a feminine end-rhyme to round things off. That feminine rhyme becomes an element in its turn; the *abab* scheme another. The semantic meaning of the words themselves is an element of the poem, as are the images they create. Were any of these elements removed in the Russian original, the poem would suffer notably. We can prove the point by attempting to provide an English paraphrase; without the rhythm or rhyme the poem seems flat, in no way beautiful; the images, presented in a literal translation, seem moreover wholly unrelated to each other, so that this unbeautiful poem is now also disjointed and nearly nonsensical (*what's some soggy page got to do with bawling infants?* the reader-in-paraphrase asks). In other words, all elements of the original poem seem to work together so simply and naturally that to remove any one of them would actually keep the others from functioning at all.

Were every element in a construction absolutely equal in importance, and reliant on every other to succeed, we would have a poem not worth the bother of failing to translate. However, I think there is an element in most of Annensky's work that is relatively unique, and which all other elements actually support in function. I propose that the best way to deal with Annensky in this circumstance—and in most circumstances—is to understand the essential unit with which he constructs his poems as being that of the *evocative phrase*, and, hence, the most important element as being the structure with which those evocative phrases are presented.

In another circumstance—an essay, for instance, by a beleaguered translator trying to make sense out of his tinkerings—an author might attempt to construct a rational argument using a succession of reasoned sentences, those reasoned sentences being *his* essential unit. Each sentence *reasons* some small argument, and, building upon each other, these reasoned arguments lead to some end, some larger, composite, arrived-at argument. John Donne writes poetry like this. In contrast, Annensky uses phrases—not sentences, but phrases, which are usually the length of the line, and which might be images, or scenarios, or, truly, just phrases in themselves—which do not *reason* but rather *evoke*, that is, evoke emotions and thoughts in the reader. As these phrases are introduced in succession, the evoked feelings build upon each other, and lead to some larger, composite, arrived-at emotion.

This is very different from what most would recognize as the normal practice of lyric poetry, and, I believe, significantly different as well from what we recognize as symbolism, at least in so far as Annensky's emotional logic is inherent in each poem and does not need any particular outside system of symbolic association to be coherent—only our shared human experience in the world.

So, if the most important element of Annensky's poem is the emotional argument made by a succession of individual evocative phrases, then it matters immensely that each individual phrase-unit be presented in the proper sense of itself, and in the proper relationship with all the other phrase-units.

This is all tragically abstract and an absolute misery to wade through, an attempt to put into words something that is instinctively grasped when dealing with Annensky. Really though, it's all just reverse engineering. We have to understand why and how Annensky works in order to put him back together. So now that we're seeing things on the blueprint that we didn't quite before, and recognize a 'most important element' where before there seemed to be none, we can start trying to re-assemble the poem in English with that element in the front of our minds.

First we notice that the individual phrase-units, while still individual, come in pairs, in line couplets where the sense of a phrase-unit only rarely crosses over the line break. In the first couplet, this understanding actually impels us to take what semantically translates as a simple idea in English— "The page always opens up the same way"—and break it apart into the two phrases as they appear across the line break in Russian, thus preserving the two 'things evoked' in the order in which they're evoked. The poem will not succeed if it begins "Drowning with ink, the page," because that is in fact the second evocative phrase in Annensky's emotional construction, and must be preceded by the idea of some yet-unspecified object which "always opens up the same to me," whose very ambiguity is central to the first 'evocation.'

Having begun the strip-tease, I'll slink out now as fast as I can; needless to say, a line-by-line examination of the rest of this poem would be largely concerned with proving me wrong in particulars. The delight of working in any structured form is exactly the moment when its limits find themselves transgressed, and this method of construction-by-evocative-phrase is no different.

ANGUISH OF REMEMBRANCE

It always opens up the same for me—
I mean the page, drowned in its black lines.
I turn away, I run from other people—
but where is there to bury me from night?

All alive are somehow far away,
everything unearthly very clear,
and long-forgotten lines blur into stains
of murky black, until the dawn appears.

I am rapt—an impossible glow;
mirage-like letters float before my eyes…
…I love when there are children home,
and all night long you hear them cry.

Innokenty Annensky, trans. Robert Isaf

Тоска припоминания

Мне всегда открывается та же
Залитая чернилом страница.
Я уйду от людей, но куда же,
От ночей мне куда схорониться?

Все живые так стали далеки,
Все небытное стало так внятно,
И слились позабытые строки
До зари в мутно-черные пятна.

Весь я там в невозможном отсвете,
Где миражные буквы маячут…
…Я люблю, когда в доме есть дети
И когда по ночам они плачут.

Osip Mandelstam's "The Valkyries" (1913-1914)

Olga Meerson

The Valkyries fly while the bows sing airs;
The cumbersome opera nears its end;
The lackeys, with fur-coats ready to hand,
Await their masters on the marble stairs.

The curtain's about to fall on it all,
Though some stray fool may still clap in the gods,
The coachmen are prancing by the fires in the cold—
Your coach is ready; all's over, no ends, no odds.

*

Летают Валькирии, поют смычки—
Громоздкая опера к концу идет.
С тяжелыми шубами гайдуки
На мраморных лестницах ждут господ.

Уж занавес наглухо упасть готов,
Еще рукоплещет в райке глупец,
Извозчики пляшут вокруг костров...
«Карету такого-то!»—Разъезд. Конец.

I translated Osip Mandelstam's poem, which was written on the very eve of World War I, because, one hundred and one years later, on the morning of the last day of 2014, my friend Izabela Grocholski was roused from sleep by Wagner's "Ride of the Valkyries" playing on the

WQXR radio station, to which her alarm clock is habitually set. She took this rather rude awakening for an ominous sign, prompting an eschatological interpretation of the historical moment in which we find ourselves—a déjà vu, of sorts, for anyone sensitive to history and its lessons. Mandelstam was himself preternaturally sensitive to his historical moment. In the early 1980s Mikhail Epstein wrote an interesting essay tracing Mandelstam's "The Valkyries" to the rather light-minded treatment of a similar vision of theatre as a model for history in Pushkin's *Eugene Onegin* (Chapter I, Stanza 22):

> Still cupids, devils, snakes keep leaping
> Across the stage with noisy roars;
> And weary footmen still are sleeping
> On furs at the theatre doors;
> There's coughing still and stamping, slapping,
> Blowing of noses, hissing, clapping;
> Still inside, outside, burning bright,
> The lamps illuminate the night;
> And still in harness shivering horses
> Fidget, while coachmen round a fire,
> Beating their palms together, tire,
> Reviling masters with their curses;
> Already, though, Onegin's gone
> To put some new apparel on.

*

> Еще амуры, черти, змеи
> На сцене скачут и шумят;
> Еще усталые лакеи
> На шубах у подъезда спят;
> Еще не перестали топать,
> Сморкаться, кашлять, шикать, хлопать;
> Еще снаружи и внутри
> Везде блистают фонари;

Еще, прозябнув, бьются кони,
Наскуча упряжью своей,
И кучера, вокруг огней,
Бранят господ и бьют в ладони:
А уж Онегин вышел вон;
Домой одеться едет он.

The parallels between Mandelstam's poem and its Pushkinian subtext are fairly obvious, so I will not recapitulate Epstein's argument here, brilliant as his close reading is. Mandelstam picks up on the motif of theatre as a symbol for catastrophic history in the making, but freights it with a new, darker significance. In place of the rather burlesque and fantastic operatic characters of Pushkin's age, Mandelstam gives us the Wagnerian Valkyries, who are not to be taken lightly. Mandelstam re-contextualizes Pushkin's motifs at a catastrophically eschatological moment in history; the implications of Mandelstam's "theatre" reach far beyond the private life of a lyrical hero like Onegin. I find this re-enactment of an opera (this time, itself a symbol of eschatological cataclysms, as is Wagner's wont) to be a very appropriate reminder to all of us, not merely my musical Polish friend, that the theatre of history may be a very grave matter—even in Pushkin's nineteenth Century, let alone Mandelstam's twentieth, or our twenty-first.

Samuil Marshak's "The Scatter-Brain from Absentminded Lane"

Jane Bugaeva, with Victoria Arend

Samuil Marshak was present throughout my childhood, as he was for most Soviet children. My mother would often recite his poetry to me—prompting many giggles. His work is filled with whimsical rhymes, nonsensical words and delightfully funny imagery. His poems are incredibly easy to remember and fun to recite—in a word, perfect children's poetry.

I was eager to share his work with English speakers and hopeful that it would bring them the same joy that it had for me. When I co-translated this work with Victoria Arend I was nervous—Victoria had never heard of Marshak, she did not speak Russian, and her only exposure to the written poem was my literal trot. But after listening to the poem in Russian, after hearing its joyful tone and playful alliterations, even without being able to understand it literally, she understood that it was something special. She could feel the poem, I could understand it, and together we were able to produce something that, I'm sure, we could not have produced individually. We channeled Marshak's whimsy and imagination in crafting our own version of this iconic poem, one that we hope is universally silly, yet clearly Russian in spirit. The collaborative experience was incredibly rewarding. Her dedication to the project was extremely meaningful to me as a translator, and her work honored to my childhood memory of Marshak.

Do you know the scatter-brain,
The man from Absentminded Lane?
He wakes up early, gets himself dressed—
He tries to look his very best.
But sometimes he fumbles, if you can believe
Since pantlegs often seem just like sleeves!
Now that's what I call a scatter-brain
The man from Absentminded Lane.

He takes a raincoat off the rack,
His wife screams, "That's mine, put it back!"
He goes to pull on his heavy galoshes,
She scolds, "Those aren't yours, they're Sasha's!"
Now that's what I call a scatter-brain
The man from Absentminded Lane.

He tries to put a hat on his head,
But grabs a frying pan instead.
He tries to kiss his wife goodbye,
But smooches the coat rack standing nearby.
Now that's what I call a scatter-brain
The man from Absentminded Lane.

He decided to go on vacation,
So off he went one day
To the nearest train station,
On a tram going that way.
Once on board, he cried to the driver,
"Most admirable tramductor,
Tram-honorable sir,
I meant to say before,
That my desired destination
Is the nearest tram,
So please stop this station
Before I get in a jam!"

The driver's jaw dropped,
And the tram stopped.
Now that's what I call a scatter-brain
The man from Absentminded Lane.

He popped into the station bar
To buy a seat in the first-class car,
And at the ticket booth, the old cashier
Was befuddled when he asked for a beer.

He ran to the platform outside,
Chose an out-of-service car for the ride,
Stowed all his luggage
In the overhead carriage;
Settled in a window seat
Then promptly fell asleep.

When he woke up, it was half-past three.
"Curious," he cried, "Where are we?"
"This is Scatterburg," was the reply
From the people passing by.

So he took another nap,
Then awoke to check back.
Outside was a crowded station,
Trying to get someone's attention,
He bellowed, "What stop is this?
Attentiveville or Wiseopolis?"
"This is Scatterburg," he was informed
From those on the platform.

So he dozed a bit more.
Waking up, he was sure
That by now he must have arrived,
So he asked the folks outside,

"Where are we now? Where have we gone?
Past Mindfulgrad? Putogetherton?"
"This is Scatterburg, can't you tell?"
From the crowd came a yell.

"What's going on?" he complained.
"Two days I've been stuck on this train,
And I'm back in Scatterburg where I started?
Like this train never even departed?!"
Now that's what I call a scatter-brain
The man from Absentminded Lane.

*

Вот какой рассеянный

Жил человек рассеянный
На улице Бассейной.

Сел он утром на кровать,
Стал рубашку надевать,
В рукава просунул руки—
Оказалось, это брюки.

Вот какой рассеянный
С улицы Бассейной!

Надевать он стал пальто—
Говорят ему: не то.
Стал натягивать гамаши—
Говорят ему: не ваши.

Вот какой рассеянный
С улицы Бассейной!

Вместо шапки на ходу
Он надел сковороду.
Вместо валенок перчатки
Натянул себе на пятки.

Вот какой рассеянный
С улицы Бассейной!

Однажды на трамвае
Он ехал на вокзал
И, двери открывая,
Вожатому сказал:

—Глубокоуважаемый
Вагоноуважатый!
Вагоноуважаемый
Глубокоуважатый!
Во что бы то ни стало
Мне надо выходить.
Нельзя ли у трамвала
Вокзай остановить?
Вожатый удивился—
Трамвай остановился.

Вот какой рассеянный
С улицы Бассейной!

Он отправился в буфет
Покупать себе билет.
А потом помчался в кассу
Покупать бутылку квасу.

Вот какой рассеянный
С улицы Бассейной!

Побежал он на перрон,
Влез в отцепленный вагон,
Внёс узлы и чемоданы,
Рассовал их под диваны,
Сел в углу перед окном
И заснул спокойным сном...
—Это что за полустанок?—
Закричал он спозаранок.
А с платформы говорят:
—Это город Ленинград.

Он опять поспал немножко
И опять взглянул в окошко,
Увидал большой вокзал,
Удивился и сказал:

—Это что за остановка—
Бологое иль Поповка?
А с платформы говорят:
—Это город Ленинград.

Он опять поспал немножко
И опять взглянул в окошко,
Увидал большой вокзал,
Потянулся и сказал:

—Что за станция такая—
Дибуны или Ямская?
А с платформы говорят:
—Это город Ленинград.

Закричал он:—Что за шутки!
Еду я вторые сутки,
А приехал я назад,
А приехал в Ленинград!

Вот какой рассеянный
С улицы Бассейной!

THE CRANES' WAY: TRANSLATING RASUL GAMZATOV'S "THE CRANES"

Irina Mashinski

HISTORY

Gamzatov wrote "The Cranes" during a visit to Japan, on the day he saw the paper cranes at the Nagasaki museum. He received the news of his mother's death on the same day. The poem was written in the Avar language, one of the languages of Dagestan, translated into Russian by Naum Grebnev, and altered by Mark Bernes, its first balladeer interpreter who famously recorded it in one session in 1969. The song later became a staple of the Soviet official repertory—sung on special occasions by soloists of military choirs and official pet singers with voices like steel pipes. It was a very Soviet—not Dagestani or Russian—song, just as Gamzatov himself, the son of the first Avar people's poet Gamzat Tsadasa, was to become the designated poet of Soviet Dagestan.

ANONYMITY

Maybe it is the complex and multilayered authorship of this text that has made it, in Soviet perception, almost anonymous, like an ancient Egyptian poem. Having lost the author's biography, the poem loses its individual poetics, too—or at least so it seems to a Russian reader. Nor does it represent an ethnographical peculiarity or a national tradition (in the final version, by Bernes, the Avar *djigits* became soldiers). It is only breadth, simplicity and height that remain. "The Cranes" is a unique case of an epic elegy.

All this added to my sense of freedom as I translated—it did not bother me much, really, that some of the feathers of the author's will were to be lost in the process. I can't say that my translation is a loose one, but I did take liberties with it.

IMAGE

I translated this poem (not the song), mesmerized by its slow solemn music, the clarity of its emotion, and its simple but piercing diction. Starting from the second stanza, I, like other readers, saw—a wedge.

DICTION

If there is anything specifically Gamzatovian in this poem, it is the adjectives.

Say, in the first stanza—*bloody* (fields) and *white* (cranes). I intended to keep these artless, slightly naive words since there they sound not like a cliché of the "Hot Love and Burning Hatred"[1] kind, but like a folk song. These adjectives are followed by others that are similarly simple, but already down-to-earth, homey: *tired* (wedge), *small* (gap). This "small" is especially moving—not only because it is so humble, but rather because it corresponds so precisely to the space that is subtracted from the earth and added to the sky. And was it Gamzatov or Grebnev or Bernes's slip of the tongue: from under the sky?

The wedge flies under the weightless heaviness of the sky above, and it is not the last freedom, either (no wonder the cranes cry out). I translated it this way:

"...beneath an evening cloud..."

POSSIBILITIES: TENSES

A wonderful possibility offered by the very nature of English grammar is the fractionality of the English past tenses, which allows one to split layers in the introduction and change the scale of the images: some

---

1   The title of Gamzatov's first collection.

The translation was first published in *The London Magazine: A Review of Literature and the Arts* (April/May 2008). The author thanks Sibelan Forrester and Alexander Veytsman for their helpful suggestions in the translation of the essay.

are zoomed in on, while others are presented in a panoramic view. However, I found that it was rhyme that, paradoxically, was the most instrumental in this translation.

POSSIBILITIES: RHYME/OFF-RHYME

Transferring a Russian rhyming scheme into English, a language tired of rhymes, has long been a painful problem, certainly a nuisance for a poet or translator who happened to have come out of the relatively young Russian poetic tradition of the 19th and 20th Centuries. Endless possibilities with words' endings in various declensions and conjugations still make Russian rhyming largely a poem-forming adventure. At the same time, in "The Cranes," rhymes add warmth to the iambic pentameter of the Russian text. A Shakespearian blank pentameter would sound way too solemn. So, everything pointed to a consonant rhyme—and in fact it is evolving spontaneously: one just needs to listen to the original. The off-rhyme in the first two stanza allows one to create an impression of a distant echo—it unfolds the sound, the plumage of the lines spreads as feathers do in a fan. Or—as cranes do in the rear-guard of a flock. The third stanza, i.e. closer to the pointed vanguard, the rhyming evens up: it becomes exact, and in the last one not just exact, but homonymic, identical. The repeated word ends the poem, so that the poem narrows, sharpens into

a wedge.

Rasul Gamzatov, trans. Irina Mashinski

A Song From Dagestan

Sometimes I think that soldiers, who have never
come back to us from the blood-covered plains,
escaped the ground and didn't cross the River,
but turned instead into white screeching cranes.

And since that time the flock is flying, narrow
or wide, or long—and maybe that is why
so often and with such a sudden sorrow
we stop abruptly, staring at the sky.

On flies the wedge trespassing every border—
a sad formation, ranks of do-re-mi,
and there's a gap in their open order:
it is the space they have reserved for me.

The day will come: beneath an evening cloud
I'll fly, crane on my right, crane on my left,
and in a voice like theirs, shrill and loud,
call out, call out to those on earth I've left.

Мне кажется порою, что солдаты
С кровавых не пришедшие полей,
Не в землю нашу полегли когда-то,
А превратились в белых журавлей.

Они до сей поры с времен тех дальних
Летят и подают нам голоса.
Не потому ль так часто и печально
Мы замолкаем глядя в небеса?

Летит, летит по небу клин усталый,
Летит в тумане на исходе дня.
И в том строю есть промежуток малый—
Быть может это место для меня.

Настанет день и журавлиной стаей
Я поплыву в такой же сизой мгле.
Из-под небес по-птичьи окликая
Всех вас, кого оставил на земле.

Translated from the Avar into the Russian by Naum Grebnev

MARIA RYBAKOVA'S *GNEDICH*, SONG III

Elena Dimov

Maria Rybakova's *Gnedich* captures the reader's attention in its first stanzas with a striking allusion to Homeric Greece: "The rage that killed so many/ the wretched rage of Achilles/who knew that he would perish/ that he would perish young." This novel about the life of Nikolai Gnedich (1784-1833)—a romantic poet, librarian, and the first translator of *The Iliad* into Russian—is written in verse, and is a fine example of the revival of the poetic tradition masterfully explored by Pushkin in *Eugene Onegin*. Like *The Iliad* itself, the novel consists of twelve Songs or Cantos, and covers the life of Gnedich from his childhood to his death.

The publication of *Gnedich* in Russia in 2011 was immediately hailed as a landmark event. The novel-in-verse received the Anthologia Prize, the "Moscow Account" Award, and the Russian Prize in short fiction, was a finalist for the NoS and the Andrei Bely Prizes, and garnered excellent reviews from both Russian and British literary critics. It depicts the lives of Gnedich and his best friend, the poet Batyushkov, who is slowly losing his sanity, and incorporates motifs from their poetry, from Homer's epics, and from Greek mythology, as well as magnificent images of imperial Russia and of the Homeric world. The space of the novel covers snowy Russian villages, aristocratic St. Petersburg salons, magnificent Italian landscapes, and austere Greece.

Rybakova conjures a fittingly romantic vision of the dramatic lives of Gnedich and his best friend. Gnedich's inner world is intense and clouded by constant melancholy; motifs from *The Iliad* invade his thoughts and transform his reality. A major part of the novel is the moving correspondence between the two poets. Philosophical reflections on the fate of the individual are intertwined with poignant stanzas devoted to the great but unhappy love that consumed both

Gnedich and his maid Elena. The novel culminates in Batyushkov's final breakdown in the lunatic asylum in Pirna and Gnedich's ruminations on Russia's tragic future fate.

The poetic language of *Gnedich* is refined: it combines the clarity of Rybakova's syllabic verses and the beauty and sophistication of her metaphors with distinct, novelistic depictions of certain landscapes, people, and their interactions. In a review in the *Times Literary Supplement*, Andrew Kahn noted Rybakova's gift for "seamlessly layering different registers, such as the vernacular of Pushkin's generation and the archaic of high-style epic," which lends a unique texture to this "winningly touching novel." This very quality presented an immensely challenging task for me as a translator: to convey the dynamics of the novel and yet retain the music of Rybakova's poetic language. The constantly changing registers in the novel led me to incorporate different linguistic modes, from the pure beauty of Homeric hexameter to an imitation of cockney jargon, which allowed me to reproduce the speech of a Russian peasant.

Gnedich is one of the most important poetic books to appear in Russian in the past few years, and its translation into English has the merit of broadening the Anglophone reader's exposure to the diversity of Russian literature. My motivation was, from the start, to convey the beauty of Rybakova's poetic style as well as the fascinating world of *Gnedich* to an English-speaking public. In my opinion, Rybakova's exquisite work represents a step forward in modern poetry, introducing new forms and themes into the poetic sphere. It is an innovative work, and deserves even more recognition than it has already justly received.

(As a last note, I would like to end this short introduction to the enthralling world of *Gnedich* with gratitude to my daughter, Margarita Dimova, for her reading and editing of the translated stanzas, to Boris Dralyuk for his helpful notes on the essay, and to my friends, who encourage and inspire me in everything.)

Cranes were crying out and jumping in front of each other—
this was the last thing he remembered before falling asleep;
but even in his sleep cranes appeared and with a cry
fell from heaven to earth, and he covered his face with his hands,
to hide it from their sharp beaks.
Their piercing cry rang out louder and louder.
He awoke and realized that somebody was knocking at the door.
The cook said a new maid would come to clean,
he said: I'll show her myself what to do,
I don't want her to wreak havoc on my papers,
but she'd better clean the dust.
The cook said: she will come.
He dresses in a robe and ties a silk scarf around his neck.

Maid, cook, friend, high court lady, loneliness,
if her dresses impeccably, clothes himself in armor—
under the cover of French fashion he fears no one.

He opens the door and sees a pale creature
of indeterminate age, who lifts her eyes at him—
almost white (*is she Finnish?*)—
but quickly lowers them (*he looks like a devil!*)
and says that she is Elena, that the cook sent 'er in,
that she she's sorry fer bein' late,
but the rope was wet and she couldn't untie the boat
'er brother olways binds 'em knots so's you can't untie 'em;
she told 'im the other day that she was goin' t' see a gentleman,
there was no way she could without the boat, they live on an island,
that's why she was late; she swears no one in town
cleans better.

He nods and makes a sign with his fingers.
She pauses, enters, he shows her to his study—
the desk he writes on, a pile of books,
a cabinet and another cabinet with a dusty smell,

an ottoman, and an armchair, and a little table,
where his pipe lies,
and in an adjacent room, the narrow bed of a bachelor,
an icon in the corner
of the Mother of God with everlasting light in front of her,
and the pale creature nods and is no longer afraid,
because if this devil keeps in his office
any devices of sorcery,
the Virgin Mary will look after her since her image is not in vain.
The featherbed is made with fine and costly linen
(*she manages to notice*); but it isn't shaken up;
and the windows are so large, but dim—they should be washed,
the light barely passes through 'em;
 he sure burns many candles, expensive, wax,
even in the daytime. These gentry are often up at night,
God knows why: one sits and sits alone by 'isself
casts a spell—who can understand 'em:
there may be icons at their home,
as though everything were normal,
but why are the rooms so huge if
they are so empty—a chair there, an ottoman here,
a desk in the corner—so much space is filled with nuffink.
He'd better get some trunk
or a cupboard with carved doors,
and the ceiling is so high—
as if a devil is flying beneath it.
(She imagines it and smiles, but then
wipes the smile from her lips so he won't think
she's laughing at him.)

He says: You'll come at noon,
because that is when I leave for my office
at the Imperial Public Library.
The words are so heavy that she kneels and bows,
when he speaks them.

I don't want even a speck of dust in the room,
nor any cobwebs in the corners—she nods—
and the books should remain in the same place

and on the same page, and the papers should not be out of order.
She nods, and he strives in vain to catch sight of
any thought on this pale face.
Well, she probably understood. Elena,
what a name for a poor maid,
but, it may be a sign that
the gods are pleased with his work of translation!

He says goodbye to her, leaves the house,
walks along the waterfront,
looks at the fishermen—one is playing a flute,
another says to him: stop it; you'll scare away all the fish,
the palaces gaze into the water, and it seems to Gnedich
that somebody is about to walk out of their front doors,
where silent lions sit turned to marble,
and call the fishermen to play the flute
to entertain the sad boyars—
but he knows there are no fairytales;
or, in any case,
where he appears—the fairytales disappear.
In the library a letter from Batyushkov is waiting for him.
He begins to read it prior to taking up the volumes.
(From one dusty book to another dusty book—
this is his path, and he himself is ash,
and dust, and an empty word).
Batyushkov writes: "What a pity you have never been to Paris.
A maze of small streets—you'd love them!
everything is measured for man in this city.
The Cathedral is great!—like a dark forest—
and stands on spidery legs.
I have been in the palace, even paid a visit to the academy.

A pity that I did not see Parny—you know,
he is my favorite.
Remember, you said once that you had dreamed a city
where everything was ugly: houses, clothes, songs,
chariots, the river, commoners, streets—
everything had sharp angles and everything was like
a wasteland, although you could still find people there.
You told me about this over a cup of coffee,
without fear of ridicule
(since only old hags
confide to each other their dreams and guess at their meaning),
you kept saying: What if such a city exists or would exist?
I have to admit that you scared me. I thought for a long time
about such a possibility and came to the conclusion
that maybe, for a minute, you had a glimpse of hell,
and that in hell our souls will be tormented by ugliness,
because the soul is not devoid of eyes,
but hell is devoid of beauty;
as for the realm of men,
I swear by our friendship, my friend Gnedko,
people will never build houses
like the ones you dreamed,
looking like boxes
which had their wrapping paper ripped off;
the soul requires beauty, it feels beauty,
the soul longs for it in the earthly vale,
it recalls what it had seen in Heaven,
as Plato teaches us,
therefore it compels hands
to raise palaces and temples,
and even in the poorest hut
to paint the window casing in azure.
That's why we love beauties and read Homer,
and listen to the violin; however, consider yourself
beloved of the gods, for it is they who let

you, my friend Gnedko, look straight into hell—
probably so that you would
translate more Greek poetry for us!
Menin aide thea peleiadeo Achileos.
So many vowels point, no doubt,
to the divine origin of the Greek language.
But I have been distracted; this is what I wanted to tell you:
get a passport for yourself and come here.
I'll show you Paris and I'll show you Germany.
If we are lucky,
we may even see Goethe.
You need to travel in the world while still young.
You've buried yourself in papers, and never show your head.
Carpe diem, as Horace says,
life passes and youth does not return."

The letter continued for two more pages.
Gnedich put it aside and opened his Homer,
but the reading was not going well, he looked out the window
through the thick glass at the city,
not the morning city but the dim one under the northern sky;
he thought: maybe I ought to go see it all,
but he knew he would not, and a tear rolled down
onto the translation and smeared the ink.
Someone saw a dragon, was startled and stopped,
in the wooded canyon in the mountains of Hellas;
his knees trembled, and he turned and ran.
Paleness spread across his cheeks: but then he himself had never
seen a dragon in the wooded ravines of his childhood.
Snakes, sometimes frogs, even lizards,
but a dragon—there was no such thing,
although he often imagined how, maybe,

a dragon was lurking in the ravine and guarding a princess,
and he, Gnedich, would go and free her, and slay the dragon.
To live and to win, one needs to get rid
of pity for the vanquished
of self-pity—but how, how
to conquer oneself?
How to see himself as nothingness,
how not to regret the fleeting days,
how to tell yourself: you're just one of many,
your job is to translate Homer,
to be loved—is not your business,
being a hero is a job for others,
and immortality belongs to the gods,
so do not pity a body, whose every part
advances toward the grave, don't pity a face
lost to disease.
Well, he agrees, he does not feel sorry for himself,
but how not to grieve for his sister—
he was not there when she was dying,
he would never forgive himself... Oh, why does life
consist only of missed farewells,
anything that might happen to me is
too small a punishment
for the blackness of my soul, hidden from all,
but known to me;
when I cannot sleep at night,
the darkness of the Lord seems so transparent,
but the blackness in my soul pours out
like spilled ink,
flooding the entire bedroom, sticks eyelashes together
and I can see neither the darkness of the Lord, nor His light.

And Elena, if it's after midnight and she is not yet asleep,
listens to mice rustling in the hall,
a lonely bird suddenly cries out in the night,
and then all falls silent—fall asleep, asleep,
into a deep and dark sleep without dreams,
like water in the well,
like the earth on a moonless night.

A little ray of light will wake you at daybreak.
It opens the flowers that had closed themselves for the night,
it stirs the feathers of the sleeping ruffled birds—
listen, birds: it's time for you to spread your wings.

At sunrise, Elena goes out,
walks barefoot in the dew,
washes up and raises her face to the sun,
her brother has not yet awoken,
and her brother's wife sleeps for a long time,
but Elena has already untied the boat
and is gliding along the river.
At noon she enters his house
with a basket and rag.
Yard keepers and cooks in this city talk about her—
no other woman cleans better,
never any complaints, clean as in paradise.
She dusts the books, wipes the shelves.
Her brother knows how to read and she could learn
from the priest in the village—but why would she?
Those book covers are dark and the scripts are weird.
She wipes the inkstand, wipes the pen—
the pen the one-eyed master's fingers had picked up,
the master's palms had touched this desk.
For the first time in her life she senses
that she wipes not just dust
but his fingers' touch;

although the master is not in these rooms,
he was there in the morning and would be in the evening,
but even now there is something of his presence:
an invisible trail, unnoticeable spirit.
She goes into the bedroom and
crosses herself in front of the icon;
begins to shake up the featherbed,
straightens the sheets, fixes a pillow,
and the imprint of a lone body
preserved from the morning
disappears.

Still she has to clean those dusty windows!
Grabbing her skirt by the hemline, she climbs onto the windowsill
with a bucket and rag, rolls up her sleeves once more
and starts to rub the glass in circles, and more circles,
wipes the sweat from her forehead, looks at the roofs
that stretch up to the Neva,
at the Admiralty Needle, at the silver water,
at the nice soft clouds;
then she starts to rub again,
and breathes on the glass,
and looks at her breath's trace
and wipes again,
so that it becomes completely crystal-clear, completely clean
in the scholarly master's apartment.

THE COMPASS TRANSLATION AWARD: RUSSIAN POETRY IN ENGLISH

This year's Compass Award competition was dedicated to the poetry of Arseny Tarkovsky (1907-89). Though he began writing in the 1920s, Tarkovsky's first collection, *Before the Snow*, did not appear until 1962, when it was praised by Anna Akhmatova as "an unexpected and precious present to the reader." Indeed, Tarkovsky was an essential bridge between the Silver Age and the generation of the Thaw. The rhythms of his verse have a mesmerizing quality. His work is both profoundly spiritual and earthy in its detail and texture. Tarkovsky's reputation among Russian poets and readers is secure, but he is only now becoming better known in the English-speaking world, which has long held his son, filmmaker Andrei Tarkovsky, in high esteem. We hope that this contest will aid in this process of discovery for English readers. After all, like the previous year's Compass poet, his friend Maria Petrovykh, Tarkovsky was himself an accomplished translator.

Below are the winning translations for the 2014 Compass Award.

Alexander Veytsman,
Compass Competition Director

Arseny Tarkovsky, trans. Laurence Bogoslaw

First Place: Laurence Bogoslaw (USA)

* * *

In autumn's final weeks, on the decline
Of bitter life,
Filled to the brim with wistfulness, I walked
Into a leafless, nameless wood.
It was engulfed from edge to edge in milk-
White fog like frosted glass. Its hoary branches
Dripped tears distilled like those
That only trees weep on the eve
Of winter that drains everything of color.
And then a miracle occurred: at sunset
Out of a raincloud peeked a gleam of blue,
A ray of light broke through, as bright as June,
A weightless spear of birdsong cast
From future days back to my past.
And now the trees stood weeping on the eve
Of noble works and festive offerings
Of cheerful whirlwinds luffing in the azure;
And bluebirds started dancing in a ring
Like hands upon a keyboard, rising measures
From earth to the highest notes the air can sing.

* * *

В последний месяц осени, на склоне
Суровой жизни,
Исполненный печали, я вошел
В безлиственный и безымянный лес.
Он был по край омыт молочно-белым
Стеклом тумана. По седым ветвям
Стекали слезы чистые, какими
Одни деревья плачут накануне
Всеобесцвечивающей зимы.
И тут случилось чудо: на закате
Забрезжила из тучи синева,
И яркий луч пробился, как в июне,
Как птичьей песни легкое копье,
Из дней грядущих в прошлое мое.
И плакали деревья накануне
Благих трудов и праздничных щедрот
Счастливых бурь, клубящихся в лазури,
И повели синицы хоровод,
Как будто руки по клавиатуре
Шли от земли до самых верхних нот.

Second Place: Nora Krouk (Australia)

THE WIND

My soul was filled with sorrow in the night.
Yet I had loved the tattered wind-lashed darkness,
stars, glimmering in flight
above wet gardens
like sightless butterflies.
The Gipsy river, a woman
In her wrap, a shaky bridge,
shawl slipping over oily sluggish water,
these helpless hands   as though before disaster.

It seemed she was alive.
Alive, as once, but moist and vowelled words
did not convey the meaning of desire
or happiness, or sorrow
and thought did not connect them any more
as is the habit there among the living.

Words burned like candles in the gusty wind
And sputtered out. As if her shoulders
Bore the grief of all. We moved, we walked
Abreast and yet her feet
Just skimmed this wormwood earth.
She didn't any more appear alive.

Once she had had a name.
September wind invades the wooden frame
now clanging locks in currents of chill air,
now flowing gentle fingers through my hair.

ВЕТЕР

Душа моя затосковала ночью.
А я любил изорванную в клочья,
Исхлестанную ветром темноту
И звезды, брезжущие на лету
Над мокрыми сентябрьскими садами,
Как бабочки с незрячими глазами,
И на цыганской масляной реке
Шатучий мост, и женщину в платке,
Спадавшем с плеч над медленной водою,
И эти руки, как перед бедою.
И кажется, она была жива,
Жива, как прежде, но ее слова
Из влажных "Л" теперь не означали
Ни счастья, ни желаний, ни печали,
И больше мысль не связывала их,
Как повелось на свете у живых.
Слова горели, как под ветром свечи,
И гасли, словно ей легло на плечи
Все горе всех времен. Мы рядом шли,
Но этой горькой, как полынь, земли
Она уже стопами не касалась
И мне живою больше не казалась.
Когда-то имя было у нее.
Сентябрьский ветер и ко мне в жилье
Врывается—то лязгает замками,
То волосы мне трогает руками.

Third Place: Igor Mazin (USA)

* * *

Forgive me, Vincent. In the very end
I could not offer you a helping hand.

I did not try to share with you your load
Nor line with grass your burned and listless road.

I did not try to soothe your weary feet,
Unlace your boots, still dusty from the street.

I did not wet your cracked lips with dew
And failed to take your gun, although I knew.

That cypress tree that never is the same,
Contorted as a twisted, tortured flame,

Your piercing-yellow chrome and Prussian blue...
How could I be myself , if not for you?

Degrading would it be for words of mine,
If I unload your burden from my spine.

And that angelic rudeness, which combines,
Your paintbrush stroke together with my lines,

Will lead us through the pupils of his eyes
To starry nights, through which Van Gogh still flies.

Arseny Tarkovsky, trans. Igor Mazin

* * *

Пускай меня простит Винсент Ван-Гог
За то, что я помочь ему не мог,

За то, что я травы ему под ноги
Не постелил на выжженной дороге,

За то, что я не развязал шнурков
Его крестьянских пыльных башмаков,

За то, что в зной не дал ему напиться,
Не помешал в больнице застрелиться.

Стою себе, а надо мной навис
Закрученный, как пламя, кипарис.

Лимоннный крон и темно-голубое,—
Без них не стал бы я самим собою;

Унизил бы я собственную речь,
Когда б чужую ношу сбросил с плеч.

А эта грубость ангела, с какою
Он свой мазок роднит с моей строкою,

Ведет и вас через его зрачок
Туда, где дышит звездами Ван-Гог.

ACKNOWLEDGEMENTS

Peter France's translations of Mandelstam appeared previously in *Poems of Osip Mandelstam*, translated by Peter France (New York: New Directions, 2014), and four of his translations of Annensky in the on-line journal *International Literary Quarterly*, 17. A significant part of Elena Dimov's translation of Maria Rybakova's *Gnedich* was published in 2013 in *Arion: A Journal of Humanities and the Classics* at Boston University.

AUTHORS

Innokenty Annensky (1856-1909) was an eminent classical scholar, translator of Euripides and for many years headmaster of the prestigious Tsarskoe Selo Lycée. He left a small body of strongly personal poetry, which was largely unknown in his life-time but was greatly admired by such poets as Anna Akhmatova and Nikolay Gumilyov.

Victoria Arend is from eastern Massachusetts. She is a French teacher and translator.

Konstantin Batyushkov (1787-1855), a member of an old noble family, took part in several campaigns of the Napoleonic wars and witnessed the destruction of Moscow. The sonorous beauty of his epicurean or elegiac poems, often influenced by French or Italian models and looking back to classical antiquity, was much admired by his younger contemporaries, including Pushkin. He succumbed to incurable mental illness and wrote almost nothing after 1822.

An uncompromising poet, prose writer, and essayst, **Ana Blandiana** (1942-) was one of the prominent voices in Romanian literature from the 1960s through the 1980s. Twice banned from publication in communist Romania for her political poetry, Blandiana expressed a wide range of feelings in highly rhetorical, confessional verse. In her early writings, her aspiration to purity conflicted with the ethical compromises of the real world; later on she reached a state of equilibrium akin to sleep, attuned to the rituals and rhythms of the natural world.

Wojciech Bonowicz (b. 1967) is an award-winning Polish poet, biographer, and journalist. He lives and works in Krakow.

Jane Bugaeva translates children's poetry and prose from the Russian.

Martín Camps (b. 1974) was born in Tijuana. After received his undergraduate degree in Mexico City he pursued graduate studies in the US and currently teaches Spanish and Latin American Literature at University of the Pacific. He is the author of four collections of poetry, including *Desierto sol*.

An anticonformist poet, anti-fascist fighter during World War Two, and co-founder of the legal communist newspaper *Scânteia* (*The Spark*), **Ion Caraion** (1923-86) subsequently spent eleven years in Romania's communist prisons (1950-55 and 1958-64). From 1964 to 1981 (when he emigrated to Switzerland), Caraion published numerous volumes of poetry, translations, personal essays, and literary criticism; he also published a journal. Marked by the horrors of the war and political detention, Caraion's poetry is often dark, sarcastic, defiant, and brutal.

Michael Casper's Yiddish translations have appeared in *The White Review* (London) and *Sephardi Lives: A Documentary History, 1700-1950*, published by Stanford University Press.

Elena Dimov was born in Vladivostok, Russia and graduated from Far Eastern Federal University with a degree in Oriental Studies. She holds a Ph.D. in Russian History from the Russian Academy of Sciences. She lived in Moscow, Hamburg, and Sofia before moving to Charlottesville, Virginia in 1999, where she works at the University of Virginia. She edits the website Contemporary Russian Literature, and her translations of Russian poetry have appeared in a number of journals and anthologies.

Boris Dralyuk is a Lecturer in Russian at the University of St Andrews, Scotland. He has translated and co-translated several volumes of poetry and prose from Russian and Polish and is co-editor, with Robert Chandler and Irina Mashinski, of *The Penguin Book of Russian Poetry* (Penguin Classics, 2015) and the *Cardinal Points* literary journal.

Piotr Florczyk is a poet, essayist, and translator. A chapbook of his poems, *Barefoot*, is forthcoming from Eyewear Publishing.

Peter France lives in Edinburgh, where he was professor of French until 2000. He has published widely on French and Russian literature and on literary translation. His translations include prose works by Diderot and Rousseau, and Russian poetry by Baratynsky, Batyushkov, Lermontov, Annensky, Mandelstam, Mayakovsky and Gennady Aygi.

Edwin Frank is the editor of the New York Review of Books Classics series. His *Snake Train: Poems 1984-2013* will come out in this spring.

Georgiana Galateanu-Farnoaga holds a PhD from Bucharest University and currently teaches Romanian language and Central European literatures and cultures at UCLA. She has published translations of Romanian prose and poetry, including *The Phantom Church and Other Stories from Romania* (University of Pittsburgh Press, 1996), which Kirkus called "A splendid collection of short fiction. [...] An exemplary anthology."

Florin Iaru (b. 1954) practices a poetry of contrasts—ironic and serious, ludic and pathetic, exuberant and nostalgic. His lyrical discourse is direct, open, and politically charged. Two of his major themes—imaginary confessions and erotic frustrations—are expressed in a colloquial language, rich in associations.

Robert Isaf is a poet, translator, and journalist from Atlanta, Georgia. He specializes in poetry from Arabic, German, Russian, and Syriac.

Maria Jastrzębska is a poet, editor and translator. Her work has been widely anthologized and her most recent collection is *At the Library of Memories* (Waterloo Press, 2013). She co-translated *Elsewhere* by Iztok Osojnik with Ana Jelnikar (Pighog Press, 2011) and co-edited *Queer in Brighton* with Anthony Luvera (New Writing South, 2014).

Alexander Kushner (b. 1936) is a well-known poet from St. Petersburg, Russia. Joseph Brodsky praised him as "one of the best lyrical poets of the 20th century."

Ilya Kutik is a renowned poet and a founder of Russian Metarealism in poetry. His poems are translated into 19 languages and included in the major anthologies of Russian poetry of the 20th century. He is the author of seven full-length collections of poetry in Russian; most recently, Epos (Moscow: Russkii Gulliver, 2011). He is also a translator of English (A. Pope, G. K. Chesterton), American (E. Pound, A. Ginsberg), Polish (C. Norwid), and Swedish (E. Stagnelius, T. Tranströmer, L. Gustavsson) poetry. He is a Professor at Northwestern University, and lives in Chicago.

Ileana Mălăncioiu (1940-) debuted in 1967, and her work since then has been marked by two themes: love, which often brings about thoughts of death, and politics. The protagonists of her erotic lyrics are half-dead, half-alive, and inhabit "the world beyond"; ritual elements from folk magic and folk tales accompany their dialogs. In her socially conscious writings, the overarching feelings are fear and the refusal to accept pervasive evil.

Osip Mandelstam (1891-1938) grew up in St Petersburg and spent some three years in Western Europe after graduating from university. A member, with Akhmatova, of the Acmeist group, he remained in Russia after the Revolution, but was increasingly at odds with the Communist regime. In 1934 he was sentenced to internal exile for a satirical poem on Stalin; living in Voronezh, he wrote a mass of remarkable verse which only survived thanks to his wife, Nadezhda. In 1938 he was re-arrested and sent to the camps, where he died the same year.

Mariana Marin (1956-2003) passed through life like a meteorite. She spread light, warmth, and compassion around her, but was herself consumed by the intensity of her poetic and personal lives. Her poetry was sincere, tragic, and direct. After the fall of communism she continued to write in the same pessimistic vein, with a deep sense of irreversible loss.

Samuil Marshak (1887-1964) was a Soviet Jewish poet and translator, renowned for his renditions of English poetry—especially Shakespeare's sonnets and the works of Robert Burns—and his brilliant children's verse.

Irina Mashinski is a bilingual poet, editor, and translator. She is the author of nine books of poetry in Russian, and her work has appeared in many journals and anthologies in both Russian and English. Irina Mashinski's English-language collection *The Naked World* is forthcoming from Spuyten Duyvil in 2015. She is the co-editor (with Robert Chandler and Boris Dralyuk) of *The Penguin Book of Russian Poetry* (Penguin Classics, 2015), as well as co-founder (with the late poet Oleg Woolf) and current editor-in-chief of the StoSvet literary project, which includes the literary journals *Storony Sveta* (in Russian) and *Cardinal Points* (in English). She received Russian America (2001) and Maximilian Voloshin (2003) Awards in poetry, and, with Boris Dralyuk, First Prize in the 2012 Joseph Brodsky/Stephen Spender Translation Prize competition.

Olga Meerson was born in 1959 in Moscow and emigrated to Israel in 1974. She subsequently moved to the United States and received her Ph.D. in Russian Literature from Columbia University. She researches and teaches on a wide range of topics in Russian literature and culture at Georgetown University, and is a translator both to and from Russian.

Azary Messerer was born in 1939. He graduated from the Moscow Institute of Foreign Languages in 1962, and worked as a journalist on Radio Moscow, the weekly newspaper *Za rubezhom*, and the magazine *Rovesnik*. After spending about three and a half years as a refusenik, he emigrated to the USA in 1981. Azary received his MA degree and PhD in Media Ecology from New York University. He then worked as a teacher in New York high schools and as a lecturer in several universities, including New York University, Boston University, and Dartmouth College. He is now teaching Writing and English Literature at Touro College.

Ken Montenegro (b. 1973) has published translations of José Eugenio Sanchez in *Skidrow Penthouse*. A native of Los Angeles, he is a widely respected writer, member of the National Lawyers Guild, and activist in the field of immigration reform and human rights.

Peter Oram (b. 1947) is a poet, painter, translator, and composer, originally from Cardiff, Wales. His works include: *Maddocks* (novel for teenagers); *The Rub* (novel); *White and Other Poems and Tease it Free* (poetry); *The Page and the Fire* (translations of Russian poetry); many books for language and music lessons in schools; two full-length musicals; and three volumes of translations of French poems by Rilke.

Lez Ozerov was a poet and literary critic of Jewish-Ukrainian origin, and a prominent name in Soviet literature in his day. He was born in Kiev in 1914, and died in Moscow in 1996. His last collection, *Portraits Without Frames*, in which he recounts intimate meetings with leading figures in Soviet life, is a sui generis poetic encyclopaedia of his era.

Juan Parra del Riego was born in Huancayo, Peru, in 1894. After traveling throughout South America and Europe, he settled in Montevideo, Uruguay, where he published four books of poetry— *Polyrhythms, Hymns of Heaven and of Railroads, White Light,* and *Carnaval Cantos*—before dying of tuberculosis in 1925.

Rikudah Potash was born in Częstochowa, Russian Poland, in 1903, and grew up in Skała. She began her career writing in Polish and later switched to Yiddish. In 1924 she moved to Łódź, where she published her first collection in 1934. That same year she moved to Palestine, where she worked as an art librarian in Jerusalem until her death in 1965.

Maria Rybakova was born in Moscow in 1973, where she attended Moscow State University before continuing her education in Germany and the USA. She is the author of several novels, beginning with *Anna Grom and Her Ghost* (1999), and the recipient of numerous literary prizes. Her most recent novel, *Chernovik cheloveka* (*The First Draft of a Human Being*) was inspired by the tragic life of the Soviet poetical prodigy Nika Turbina.

José Eugenio Sánchez (b. 1965) was born in Guadalajara and now resides in the northern state of Monterrey. His playful and irreverent poetry is widely anthologized. His collection *Physical Graffiti* was particularly popular in Mexico.

Anthony Seidman has published poems and translations in such publications as *World Literature Today, Nimrod, The Bitter Oleander, Beyond Baroque, Slipstream, The Black Herald Review*, and *Ambit*. Last year, Piedra Cuervo press of Tijuana, Mexico, published his translations of Roberto Castillo Udiarte in the collection *El blues del cuervo*. His second collection of poetry, *Where Thirsts Intersect*, is still available from The Bitter Oleander.

César Silva Márquez (b. 1974) was born and raised in Ciudad Juárez, Mexico. His works include the poetry collection *ABCDario* and the novel *Una isla sin mar*. He currently resides with his family in Veracruz.

David Shook is a poet, translator, and publisher whose first collection of poems, *Our Obsidian Tongues* (2013), has just been released in paperback by Eyewear in London. He lives in Los Angeles.

Yevgeniy Sokolovsky was born in Kiev, Ukraine and moved to the United States in 1992. He graduated from Columbia University, where he pursued a major in Russian Literature and a concentration in Mathematics. Currently he works as an academic librarian at Berkeley College, New Jersey.

Tristan Tzara (1896-1963) is best known in Romanian and European literature as the co-founder of Dadaism (1916) and an author of both Dadaist and Surrealist poetry. He began his career, however, as a Symbolist epigon, debuting in the journal *Simbolul* (1912). In his early poems Tzara ironizes the conventions of traditional nineteenth century poetry, miming naïveté, infantilism, and "boarding school" nostalgia and languor.

Alexander Veytsman was born in Moscow in 1979. Alexander writes poetry, fictional prose, and essays. He also translates poetry into English and Russian, having worked with the verse of Constantine Cavafy, Joseph Brodsky, Mark Strand, and Glyn Maxwell, among others. Alexander is a graduate of Harvard and Yale universities. He lives in New York City.

Starting as a Symbolist poet, **Ion Vinea** (1895-1964) moved on to Modernism and to a moderate Avant-gardism. He debuted in 1912, in the journal *Simbolul* (*Symbol*), which he had co-founded with Tristan Tzara and Marcel Iancu; in 1919 he founded the journal *Contimporanul* (*The Contemporary*), which served as a launching pad for Modernist and Avant-gardist poetry. *The Hour of Fountains*, a volume gathering poems he had published in periodicals throughout his life, appeared in 1964, shortly after his death.

Vladimir Vysotsky (1938-1980) was a legendary Soviet Russian singer, songwriter, poet, and actor of mixed Jewish and Russian descent whose career had an immense and enduring effect on Russian culture.

Anton Yakovlev is originally from Moscow, Russia, and now lives in Ridgewood, New Jersey, where he works as a college textbook editor. He studied filmmaking and poetry at Harvard University and has directed several short films. He is the author of *Neptune Court* (The Operating System, 2015).

Olga Zaslavsky, Ph.D., is a Davis Center Associate at Harvard University. She is a literary scholar and translator of prose and poetry. She is grateful to Miles Rind, Ph.D., for his help with editing her translation of Alexander Kushner's poem.

The StoSvet Press publishing house is a part of the
US-based StoSvet project,
which also includes the *Стороны Света / Storony Sveta*
and *Cardinal Points* literary journals, the «Union "I"» web portal,
and the annual Compass Translation Award.

Founding director: Oleg Woolf (1954 – 2011)
Editor: Irina Mashinski
www.stosvet.net

One can order this or other books published
by StoSvet Press directly from its
web-site www.StoSvet.net/lib/ or by
sending an e-mail to info@stosvet.net

This volume of *Cardinal Points* was published
in conjunction with MadHat Press:
www.MadHat-Press.com

www.ingramcontent.com/pod-product-compliance
Lightning Source LLC
Chambersburg PA
CBHW031250090426
42742CB00007B/388